Beyond Nice

Creating Excellent Working Relationships in Churches and other Christian Organisations

MARTIN WOODROOFE

Copyright © 2013 Martin Woodroofe.

All rights reserved. No part of this book may be reproduced, stored, or transmitted by any means—whether auditory, graphic, mechanical, or electronic—without written permission of both publisher and author, except in the case of brief excerpts used in critical articles and reviews. Unauthorized reproduction of any part of this work is illegal and is punishable by law.

ISBN: 978-1-4834-0218-5 (sc)
ISBN: 978-1-4834-0217-8 (e)

Because of the dynamic nature of the Internet, any web addresses or links contained in this book may have changed since publication and may no longer be valid. The views expressed in this work are solely those of the author and do not necessarily reflect the views of the publisher, and the publisher hereby disclaims any responsibility for them.

Any people depicted in stock imagery provided by Thinkstock are models, and such images are being used for illustrative purposes only. Certain stock imagery © Thinkstock.

Lulu Publishing Services rev. date: 07/11/2013

Table of Contents

PART ONE

Chapter 1	The Number One Issue	3
Chapter 2	Relationships	13
Chapter 3	Agendas and Alignment	31
Chapter 4	Human Leaders and Human Followers	45
Chapter 5	Accountability	67
Chapter 6	Distrusting Professionalism	81
Chapter 7	Growth	95
Chapter 8	Volunteerism	107

PART TWO

Chapter 9	What Did Jesus Do?	121
Chapter 10	Authority and Expectations	125
Chapter 11	Tough Love	131
Chapter 12	Confronting Difficult Issues	137
Chapter 13	Humility and Resolve	143
Chapter 14	Personal Responsibility	145

PART THREE

Chapter 15	The Interviews	151
Chapter 16	Get Aligned	155
Chapter 17	Healthy Relationships	167
Chapter 18	Hire Great Leaders	181
Chapter 19	Support Your Leaders	199
Chapter 20	Use Good Tools	209
Chapter 21	Grown up Volunteering	221
Chapter 22	Negotiation	229
Chapter 23	Conclusion	241

Bibliography *245*

PART ONE

CHAPTER 1

The Number One Issue

The paradox

CHRISTIAN ORGANISATIONS, WHETHER they be churches, para-churches, charities or other bodies should be great at the people and relational side of things. This should be a key strength of any Christian organisation because as Christians we are united by a common faith and we regard each other as brothers and sisters in Christ. Because of this, our relationships should be more loving, more open, more honest and more supportive than any secular organisation. Our core purpose, spreading the good news about Jesus Christ, should unite and focus us, and the bible's teaching should mean that ideas and practices like accountability and authority are easily accepted and enacted.

However, paradoxically, we often struggle with the people issues and find it hard to get this part of our organisations right. Relationships are not always what they should be, unity is often lacking and downright division can be present. Indeed, we often seem to manage the people part of things much more poorly than the secular world. Good businesses continually invest in how they manage their people. They ensure their people understand the company's purpose and are aligned to it, they ensure that people get good feedback and recognition, and that they understand their roles and what's expected of them. They also ensure that difficult issues are tackled in a timely manner!

So what's going on in Christian bodies and why do we find it so hard to run the people side of our organisations? Well this is a big question and one that we will explore together in this book. I will try to unpack some of the challenges we face by sharing the experiences, and frustrations, which seem to be very common in many Christian organisations. Hopefully these experiences will point to some of the things that make it tough for us to manage people issues effectively.

Often we'll see that we are trying so hard to do the *'nice' thing* that we end up <u>not doing</u> the *'right' thing*. Our intentions are often (not always) good but sometimes this means we don't do what is right and necessary. In many instances doing the right thing can mean confronting difficult issues and behaviour. Again, we sometimes find this hard to do, especially as we want always to be, and to be seen to be, loving and supportive communities.

As we will see there are many things that make it difficult for Christian organisations to tackle the people issues, but before considering these we have to acknowledge that we come to this issue, like all others, as imperfect people. There's an interesting piece of data which shows that the use of pornographic TV channels in hotel rooms is no different during a Christian conference than during a conference by any other group—that is it's equally high! As people, we are still 'work in progress.' We're not yet perfect and we're inevitably going to make some very human mistakes.

The elephant in the room

Leading and managing people, and also how people behave and relate to each other, is a huge issue for Christian organisations. In fact the Christian leaders I interviewed for this book put it as *the number one challenge* they face. It's an issue which often absorbs huge amounts of time, especially leadership time, and which can lead to great negativity and the deterioration, or even break down, of relationships. Even where this does not happen, it seems that a lack of good people management means that very able people achieve less than would normally be expected.

However, in spite of this, the issue is often not acknowledged and the people issues, especially people problems, are frequently not addressed. Perhaps the main reason for this is that these issues are tough. Not only does it take a consistent and sustained effort to address them effectively, but tackling them can involve some kind of confrontation; this can take the form of confronting unacceptable or disruptive behaviour. Because of this, many times we just hope that if we ignore them they will go away! So, this issue is the elephant in *our room*—it's big and significant, and we often don't tackle it. The result of this is that we see *blockages* emerge in Christian organisations. In turn, these blockages mean that we're prevented from fulfilling our mission as effectively as we could.

As a Christian I believe Christian work is the most important thing people can do. By this I mean the making the good news of Jesus Christ and God's plan for our salvation known. This work can take many forms, but full time Christian ministry is a special form. Through this we look to help others understand God's love for them, the wonder of Jesus' sacrifice on the cross, and ultimately we hope to help people find eternal salvation by introducing them to faith.

Given this significance, it seems self evident that we should be looking to do all we can to run effective organisations, to manage our people issues as well as we can, and at least as well as the very best secular organisations. If companies are continually investing in how they manage their people in order to deliver better profits and shareholder value, then shouldn't we be willing to become as good as possible in this area? Our 'profit' and 'shareholder value' is the priceless gift of eternal life. In this way we can better serve God and fully utilise our talents for kingdom building work.

The huge upside

So, we're not always as good at the people part of things as we should be and we often fail to tackle this key issue.

Fortunately that's not the whole story! It is also true that we have a huge upside in that we have the opportunity to run the people side of things a lot better than the secular world. We do face challenges, and we do create some burdens for ourselves, but we also have the clearest possible purpose, we can have the best relationships and community, and we have faith. Our clear purpose—sharing the good news about Jesus Christ and undertaking kingdom building work—means that we can harness the huge enthusiasm, energy and passion which people bring to this work.

If we build the communities we are capable of building, in ways we are called to, then we can enjoy a level of support, honesty and openness that it's hard to see anywhere else. We can certainly avoid the politics, power struggles and mixed motives that are seen in some secular bodies. Finally, through faith, we know that we can achieve much more than is humanly possible, and more than even the mightiest corporation can dream of.

The fact is that we have everything going for us provided we do not construct our own blockages and then reinforce them.

Crucially, we also have Jesus' own example of how to interact with, lead and serve people; we will be taking a look at this in the book. In scripture we have the best roadmap possible but we need to get this map out and look at it and we need to apply the lessons (even the tough ones) that it gives us.

There's another source of encouragement. During the course of my research for this book, I talked to many Christian leaders. People who are leading highly acclaimed organisations, both churches and charities. I also talked with many experienced and able business leaders—leaders who are committed Christians and have a heart to see Christian organisations be real communities which are as effective as possible in fulfilling their mission. These people told very similar stories and offered similar advice as to how Christian bodies could address their people issues and build great organisations. I have tried to distil this advice in the book and I hope that it provides encouragement and some useful ideas for your organisation.

Everyone seems to agree that the difference between running things well and struggling is not a million miles apart; rather it's only a few short strides. Consider if you will an oil tanker heading in one direction, if it turns only 10 degrees, in a thousand kilometres it will have changed its course by 90, 100, or even 120 degrees. This idea, that a 10% change can make a 100% difference is one that I find very encouraging. Small improvements can lead to a massive overall improvement in performance over time. So the task of tackling the people issues is not insurmountable, but you do have to start on the journey of change and you do have to be willing to go through some pain.

The spiritual blockage

I said earlier that Christian work is the most important work that we can engage in, concerned as it is with eternal salvation. It is because of this that many believe we face additional blockages to being successful. These are spiritual blockages and challenges beyond our normal human experience.

I believe this is true and that because of this we must keep our eyes on God and must submit our plans and endeavours to Him in prayer. We must seek God's protection and His will in all we do.

Having said this I don't think we should get debilitated by believing that everything is related to a spiritual battle and that because of this we are powerless and can not make a difference. God gave us the ability to make choices and He expects us to make these wisely and do the best we can. He also gave us common sense and talents and again I think He expects us to fully deploy these in His service. So whilst we should be aware that there is a spiritual dimension to our work, we should not let this debilitate us and make us leave our brains and abilities outside our churches, charities and other Christian bodies!

Who's to blame?

We all know that there are frustrations in being part of a Christian community and like all people everywhere we sometimes think that someone else is the key cause of these.

If only the leaders were stronger, clearer, more willing to address problems, or more compassionate, better listeners, more spiritual then all would be OK. If only the leadership group were better organised or better connected, or more supportive of the pastor then all would be OK. If only people would just behave as we do then all would be OK!

Well it's not just a Christian cliché to say that we all have our part to play in building the organisation we want, and if we're not careful we can all play a part in tearing it down. We often do this latter thing by pursuing what we passionately believe is right. In fact we believe it's so right that we are prepared to go to war with those who disagree, and will continue this war whatever the cost because we are so convinced of the justness of our cause!

Because of this, the book is for *all* members of Christian organisations. In our different roles, leaders and led, we can positively and negatively influence the character and behaviour of our organisations. This book is an attempt to look at why we face people challenges, why this is different to the secular world, and what solutions are available to us. These solutions are taken from the life and ministry of Jesus, and also from today's highly regarded and effective Christian organisations.

Just who are you?

I thought I would ask the question many of you may be asking by now—who are you to be offering a view and advice in this area?

Well in the area of people management I have spent a quarter of a century in human resources for major commercial companies, and have operated internationally for more than 10 years. I have spent six years as a church elder of an English-speaking, bible-believing church in Brussels, during which time we have experienced our usual and fair share of blessings and challenges. I also led a 10,000 member-strong national voluntary organisation in my youth, and I am now a trustee of a major charity linked to the Anglican Church. We will see a part of our people challenge and opportunity is the voluntary nature of much of our work and support.

I therefore come to this issue with a Christian and business background and an experience of many organisations. Indeed it is this combination of experience in business and in the Christian world that made me want to write this book. I wondered why running the people side of things was so difficult in a Christian context, and was in fact more difficult than in the secular business world.

In addition to my own experience, I also recognized the need to seek out the views of those working in the Christian field. I wanted to engage their experience and wisdom, so I have based much of the book on a series of interviews. These interviews were with people who have extensive knowledge of Christian organisations and the challenges involved in leading them. They are pastors, Christian charity leaders, informed laity, consultants in this space and academics. These are the genuine experts and to all of these I should like to extend my heartfelt thanks for all the time, wisdom, encouragement and insight they gave.

During the interviews I found it interesting to see how many people expressed the challenges in the same or similar ways and also pointed to the same kind of solutions. There were of course differences of emphasis and approach but many of the core ideas were the same whether the person was running a church or not, and regardless of nationality, and in the case of the charities, regardless of the field they were operating in.

Frustrations and purpose

I am sure that anyone who is a member of a Christian community has, at some time, felt very frustrated with that community. This frustration can have a huge variety of forms; it can be that we expect the community to be perfect but we see a lot of non-perfect behaviour around us, it can be that the community seems more inward looking and less welcoming than we expected. If we've been involved for some time it can be that it seems to take forever to get things done.

We can also be frustrated that corrosive issues are being ducked and not tackled. It might be that we're frustrated that we seem to have the same debates time and time again and nothing moves forward. It might be that our administrative processes are poor and that we think our paid staff are indulging their own work preferences rather than getting on with what they need to do. It could be that we have unresolved divisions, and that we think the teaching, music, or seating could all be better!

Feeling frustrated and becoming very passionate (angry?) about it is not unusual. These frustrations more often than not stem from human interactions and shortcomings—including our own. They add to the sense that in Christian circles we often struggle with the people side of things.

So what is really going on? Let's now try and take a look at this together and see why we often find this issue so tough. We'll also consider in parts 2 and 3 of this book how the challenges can be tackled and how we can get our organisations to a better place.

Just before we do this, some people have suggested to me that big organisations are likely to tackle their people management better than small ones. I considered making this a special section in the book but my recent observations would be that this is sometimes true due to greater resources and a greater number of professionals but not always so. In view of this I have decided to view both small and large organisations in the same way i.e. having the same challenges, and definitely benefiting from the same solutions.

CHAPTER 2

Relationships

Relationships are central

IN ANY CHRISTIAN organisation, relationships are likely to be central. As Christians we value fellowship, we want to build community and we believe in the importance of trying to act as a family. This can give a real strength to our communities. From it we can gain a strong sense of belonging and a unique and positive sense of a loving community. However, the centrality of relationships can also provide us with some real challenges when it comes to actually *running an organisation and getting it to perform*.

My experience, and that of many of the people I talked to, was that for some people relationships are so central that they become an end in themselves. The thinking becomes that if we have good relationships and a loving community then we have achieved what we set out to do. Relationship can become more important than seeing the organisation achieve its stated objectives. Having a positive community is obviously highly important but it can be destructive if this is all we aspire to. If a church is so satisfied or absorbed with its existing church family that it loses focus on evangelism, it's unlikely to be fulfilling its mission. If a charity becomes all about its own community and not about serving the group it was founded to minister to, it's unlikely to be fulfilling its mission.

Now this may seem like an extreme case but we see it all around us in our organisations. People would not identify it as starkly as this. They would *not say* that community is more important than anything else, but they often transmit this message by their actions, what they focus on, and what absorbs their time and energy. In subtle ways many feel that community is what they have signed up for, and if this is OK then it is not necessary to worry too much about what gets done, if it gets done and how it gets done.

How we are can seem more important than what we do—being becomes more important than doing. Indeed community may be where our hearts are. Being part of a good community can be very personal in that it meets our needs, so of course we want it to be central. This feeling may also be present in some of the paid staff who may feel that this is what they signed up for and, more relevantly, what they were searching for when they made the professional move from the secular world.

This centrality of relationships looks different to the secular world and the business organisation. Whilst businesses do want to build good teams, a positive culture and united company, it's highly unlikely that any business could allow the community to trump its mission. If it did it would almost certainly fail to fulfil its objectives and go broke! They would recognise that good community is most effective when married to a clear mission which people are focused on fulfilling.

Relational complexity

In the Christian world, relationships are not only central they can also be complex. This is also the case in the secular world, but in Christian organisations there is a further complexity. This is derived from the fact that people often have multiple, and very different, roles when interacting with each other. To illustrate this, let's take the example of a church leader and a staff member.

At different times the leader's relationship and role with the staff member might be anything from brother or sister in Christ, to pastor, to boss. Different circumstances may legitimately demand all these roles. Now the challenge is whether the leader and staff member can recognise that different roles apply in different situations. Can they understand that whilst they have shared and prayed together, whilst their families are close, whilst they are members of the same community there will also be times when one of them is the boss and the other the subordinate? A boss who will be setting objectives and standards, and not only setting these things but also holding the other person accountable for delivering against these objectives or behaving in an acceptable way.

In Christian organisations there seem to be times when these multiple 'hats' can paralyse or baffle both the leaders and the led. These are often times when difficult issues have to be tackled. In these circumstances the person being led often expects some special dispensation 'we've prayed together so I don't expect you to raise any tough issues with me' and the leader can be confused about whether he or she is meant to approach the issue as boss, pastor, or buddy. I have had related to me occasions when this means that the issues are tackled half-heartedly, or when the leader has tackled the matter by trying to be all things to the person they are dealing with *at the same time!*

As can be imagined this leads to a real 'dog's breakfast' of messages and will probably mean that neither party is really satisfied with how the issue has been addressed and the interaction they've had.

Christian leaders need to play all these roles, however boundaries need be set in each circumstance. When dealing with a person the leader must make it clear what the context is, and explain which role is operating at that given moment. This does not mean the pastoral concern is left outside the room, but it does mean that everyone is clear as to what is taking place and what the context is. Bill Hybels sums this up neatly, saying, 'I am always your pastor and sometimes your boss'.

As a final word on role complexity, we also have to consider that unfortunately it is also not unheard of that some Christian leaders can use this role ambiguity to duck their leadership job.

They will say that they are called to be the teacher and pastor of the community, and because of this they cannot also be the leader and boss. The difficulty of this stance can be seen in any church with a significant membership. Any such organisation is a complex body needing leadership, and it is unlikely that anyone apart from the senior pastor can assume this role. People want their main leader (i.e. the pastor in this context) to lead and do not want to have to deal in this regard with other 'less senior' individuals.

In fairness, many Christian leaders are seeking to duck this leader/boss role as they have never been equipped to fulfil it. Their training did not cover the nature of effective leadership, or the tools needed to fulfil this role. In fact many were not even told that this role would be required of them!

Confronting the difficult

The centrality of relationships in Christian organisations, added to a desire to demonstrate the love of Christ, can often mean that we believe everyone must be kept 'in the boat' or remain part of the community at any cost.

It is of course understandable that Christian bodies want to keep people as part of the community. At our core we are concerned for the salvation of others and want people to be encouraged in their faith through community

This desire to keep people in the 'family' can be in spite of the way they behave and no matter how difficult they become. I am sure we can all think of cases where people move from being the 'grit in the oyster' to being really uncooperative and destructive. 'Grit in the oyster' people have questions and challenges for the leadership, but normally they want to keep things sharp and get to a better outcome through challenge and debate. This is healthy and I would encourage organisations to treasure and value these people; they often drive better outcomes. The responsibility of these folks is to challenge and prod in a gracious and helpful way, not merely to be the people who stand on the riverbank and throw rocks at those trying to row the boat.

However, sometimes people move beyond this condition to being destructive. They want to tear down all ideas, have their own way at the expense of others, demand huge amounts of time and attention, and refuse to co-operate with the wider community.

Now sometimes our desire to be inclusive and caring means that we sacrifice the need to tackle and confront this kind of behaviour. We seem to lose the ability to speak 'the truth in love' or as one person graphically put it, 'honesty gets pulped in the relationship crusher'. Given this we can shy away from doing what is right and also leave unaddressed many issues which then grow out of all proportion and come back to bite us.

Many of us will have experienced situations in our lives where issues that were not addressed grew in size and out of all proportion. As a consequence something that could have been dealt with fairly easily at the beginning requires huge amounts of time and energy to deal with in the end.

A common example of this I uncovered is where unacceptable behaviour of a staff member could and should be addressed early on. The leader should talk to the person, identifying the problem and outlining what changes they need to see and how these will be monitored. The leader should also make it clear that change is required, and that failure to do this will force the organisation down the path of dismissal. However the central problem is often not tackled and all sorts of people try to help—without addressing the central issue of unacceptable behaviour. The issue then takes on a life of its own as other people get involved, share their opinion and take sides. The result of all this will be that the whole thing escalates out of all proportion.

Furthermore, the fact that this person's unacceptable behaviour is not being addressed becomes debilitating and confusing for other members of staff. They become angry and frustrated that the issue is not tackled in a clear and straightforward way, that their leaders are hiding from the issues and not demonstrating the kind of leadership they want.

The family aspect

Unlike the secular world, most Christian organisations have the characteristics of a family and an organisation at the same time. This is a real strength but can also provide a relational challenge for us. A senior pastor once described to me how people would sometimes use these different relationships (family and organisation) to assist their own cases.

There were some staff members who, when faced with difficulties about their own performance, wanted the rules of a family to apply. Rules they saw as meaning that they would comforted, coaxed and encouraged, rather than being confronted and challenged or measured, which they saw as somehow secular. Alternatively, when they wanted resources to expand their ministry area they often looked for the rules of an organisations to apply. Rules like resource generation, and allocation.

This again is a bit like the issue of relational complexity that we looked at earlier. We need to be clear how we are operating at any given time, so to paraphrase, 'we are always a family and sometimes we need to act like an organisation.'

One other way we see this family aspect is that in many churches or other Christian bodies there are a high number of people who will always expect the rules of family to apply. Given this they are distressed when they see their leadership disciplining a person or being clear and demanding when dealing with a tricky issue. Somewhere in their own minds it seems that they believe that a demand for excellence and high standards cannot live with a compassionate 'family orientated' disposition.

Seventy times seven

In Christian bodies we tend to (rightly) work hard to protect individuals. This extends to giving them second, third, and fourth chances when there is a problem. Indeed the bible talks of seventy times seven chances, Matthew 18:22.

As a result of this, there are many times when the wider body cannot and should not know the details of the performance or behavioural issue that is being tackled. This predominantly applies to paid staff but can also apply to volunteers in key roles. The leadership often has to keep this information to themselves in order to protect the person they are managing.

However, as the wider body is not aware of all the facts they can often jump to conclusions, and not fully understand why the leadership is being tough and demanding in handling an individual. This lack of knowledge can mean that the leadership team experiences a lot of challenge, emotion and even hostility from their wider membership.

Take the example of Patrick. As a church leader Patrick is particularly passionate about some aspects of his ministry and devotes himself to this area. As a result, those in this area think he is excellent, indispensable, and doing a great job. However, what they don't see is that this area is only 20% of what Patrick was hired to do. He is not attending his other duties and indeed is not attending the key area he was taken on to look after. This is causing both strains and stress on the rest of the leadership team as they know Patrick is being overly rewarded for what he is actually doing. They need to take this issue on but also know that his admirers will be incensed and vocal. They also know that those who are not getting his time (and know this) are unlikely to be very public about this. They want the leadership to tackle the issue but don't want to get 'in the firing line' themselves.'

The leadership now needs to address this issue and either correct Patrick's behaviour in his current role, or get him to move on. In order to protect his reputation, they also need to do this without explaining to everyone that he is not pulling his weight. They have to confront this issue with him, but are unlikely to want to be public about it. This is about protecting him and giving him another chance.

It's also not impossible that Patrick will *not* help out. He may play, either intentionally or unintentionally, to the wider body for sympathy and support rather than facing up to and working through his issues. Often this lobbying of the wider body is done quite subtly, by dropping hints or by not correcting inaccurate views expressed by others. This can make the wider body think Patrick is a victim, and their reaction can help reinforce his own view that this is in fact true!

This is a real dilemma, to deal with a person without being able to talk about the issues to a wider group. It's one we face as we seek to protect people but also deal with unacceptable behaviour. In such cases, leaders need to build trust with their people over time and the wider community has to trust them to deal with these issues. This trust is crucial, especially when not everyone can or should see the whole picture.

Being too nice

In being part of a Christian community I imagine that many of us want to operate in an atmosphere where we feel that compassion and forgiveness are fully demonstrated. This seems to be a real driver in many Christian communities, and it is to be cherished.

However, there are times when our desire to promote compassion and forgiveness means that honesty and the ability to promote real relationships can be lost.

What do I mean by this? Well it appears that because we want to be compassionate we won't be honest with people. As a result of this we can end up treating them like children. Let's take a look at this through Linda's case.

Linda is underperforming in her role. She's employed as the key administrator for a church and feels that her role is undertake a series of set administrative tasks, and to devote any time 'left over' to building relationships and chatting to those who come in and out of the office. She feels that by doing this she is creating the right atmosphere in the church office. Unfortunately, this means that she does not own the wider administrative needs of the church and the clergy, in addition to their other duties, have to pick up much of the administration. Linda does not see the need to take this off their shoulders and to build an effective team of volunteers who can help out with routine and occasional administrative tasks. Indeed her focus is so much on her own, limited area of work that she feels that this fully takes up her time and she does not step-up to take on the many other tasks that should fall to her.

Because people don't want to hurt her feelings no one addresses this issue with her. People think they are being loving, respectful and supportive by not sharing this with her, although they are sharing their frustrations with each other! They can see she is underperforming and is expecting the clergy and volunteers to do much of what she should naturally be doing.

In this situation the organisation is treating Linda a little like a child, and creating a lot of problems for itself. It thinks it is being compassionate by not confronting the issue with her, but is actually being disrespectful by not engaging in a 'grown up' discussion about the situation.

Her boss is trying to be compassionate and understanding but ironically, by being too nice he is not helping her or the organisation. In fact he should respect Linda enough to be able to operate a little 'tough love'. That is he should be thinking, 'I respect you enough to be honest and open about the issue with you. I want to address this issue so we can move forward together, and I want to address it grown up to grown up.'

In the end this is going to be a more respectful and loving approach. We have to be careful that by being too nice we don't end up treating people as less than ourselves. We also have to be careful that we don't underestimate them, thinking that they will not be able to understand the problem and work through possible solutions.

Underperformance is difficult, but we owe it to Linda to explain the real job she should be doing. We owe it to her to explain what we need her to do and the standards that must be met, and we then need to give her a chance to do the job properly. It may be simply that she has not done this as no one explained the parameters of the role or was clear with her about what she was expected to do and how she was expected to do it.

Linda may well accept the situation when it's put to her and may be willing to work to a level that suits the organisation. It may also be that she does not want to operate in such a demanding role, in which case it may well be better for her and the organisation if she steps down and allows someone better suited to be recruited into the position. The alternative is we leave a 'running sore' as we're not willing to address another person on equal terms. A running sore, which hurts the organisation and the person involved.

Ironically, our shared faith should help us to be more honest with each other, but often niceness and a belief that everything in the garden must *appear* rosy leads us to duck being honest and to dumb down our relationships. Funnily enough it is unlikely that we would be prepared to do this in the rest of our lives so it seems a little strange that we would do this in a Christian context, not only a little strange but not actually scriptural as well. The bible says where you have a problem with your brother you are required to go an address this with him (Matthew 18:15), not to duck it and pretend all is well.

There is a further challenge in being too nice. Not only may we be treating people as less than ourselves but also we may not be doing them any favours. In many cases in my working life I have encountered people who are square pegs in round holes, i.e. they were doing jobs which did not suit them but reasons of security led them to hang on to these roles. In the vast majority of cases when this was confronted and the person either moved on from the organisation, or within it, they got a fresh lease of life and an opportunity to be successful. Many looked back at this difficult time as the prelude to their life getting better and their work performance and satisfaction going to much higher levels as they moved into more suitable roles.

Secular relationships

Set against the Christian challenges let's consider relationships in many secular organisations. Secular organisations, especially businesses, can often have a lot more clarity about relationships. People can have very good personal relationships that have been built up over a number of years of working together. Despite this, in the end it's clear to everyone that they have to fit with the organisation and work to achieve its goals—generally if you don't do this you get fired. In such organisations, if there is a conflict between what the individual wants and what the organisation wants then everyone tends to revert back to the needs to the organisation. People generally have to fit in or 'ship out'. This may sound harsh, but it can create clarity for people about where they stand, and can also create an honesty and straight forwardness that we sometimes miss.

Generally, no one likes confronting difficult issues, be they in the Christian or secular world. Simply put, it's painful and we know emotional energy is going to be used up in the process. Sometimes people are even *fearful* of these conversations, the last thing they want to do, or feel equipped to do, is sit down and tackle a problem face to face. Indeed in the course of my interviews it has become apparent that many Christian leaders can have this feeling, especially as many of them feel a high degree of vulnerability in their role. They can find the feedback they receive is painful, and as a consequence don't want to hurt others by giving feedback on performance, or behaviour. They may also not want to have to engage in the on-going difficult discussions that may emerge from confronting tricky and unacceptable situations.

So it is true in all organisations, be they companies, governmental bodies, charities or churches, that confronting difficult issues is not something they relish. However this is made much more challenging when there are no systems and processes for tackling difficult issues, and very little experience of how to manage these situations.

Good secular organisations have generally put a lot of time and effort into this area. They especially focus on managing performance, and so whilst people still find this a tough area to deal with, at least there is good process and experience to draw upon. Many Christian organisations do not enjoy the systems, culture or training to be able to engage with confronting the unacceptable.

This lack of skill in the area of performance management and conflict resolution can also have a major unintended consequence for Christian bodies. This unintended consequence seems to be that when the problem eventually becomes so great that it has to be dealt with, it is often managed in a very heavy-handed way. We spend a long time not addressing the issue and then go overboard and tackle it in a 'nuclear' manner. Generally, there is a heavy price to pay for this response. A heavy price in terms of broken relationships, damaged credibility and divided opinions.

What does all this mean for me?

Hopefully you will have recognised and agreed with some of the ideas and observations in this chapter, and I also hope it has illuminated a few areas which may have be challenging you and your team but you weren't sure why. However, in order to provide additional help I want to offer an analysis tool and a real story in each of the chapters in part one of this book—in these chapters we look at the problems Christian organisations encounter. In part three (the solutions part) we'll do the same thing but these models will be focused on providing solutions more than generating analysis of the issues.

These tools are offered so that you might take a look at whether the topic highlighted is an issue for your organisation. Being aware of this is the first step to being able to tackle it.

Analytical tool:

If you want to check out if your organisation has a clearly understood mission and is focused on this, or if this has been 'crowded out' by other considerations like making relationships central then one way you might examine this is by using a small focus group.

This group could be formed from your leadership or you could deliberately take a cross section of your population. The latter approach might well be more revealing as you will be tapping into the thinking of people who might not normally be drawn into such a discussion. Keep the group to a manageable size where people will be willing to speak up, between eight and twelve, and try and allow a few hours for the event.

In terms of what you want them to consider divide your groups into smaller groups and ask them to work on the following questions:

> Mission and Goals – 30 minutes

- What are the mission and goals of our organisation?
- Does everyone know these? (scale of 1 to 5, 1 being no one has a clue about them and 5 being everyone knows them)
- Does everyone know what they are responsible for in terms of achieving our mission and gaols? (scale of 1 to 5, 1 being no one has a clue and 5 being everyone knows what they are responsible for and have to do)
- Do people feel equipped to fulfil their responsibilities with regard to the mission and goals? (scale of 1 to 5, 1 being people don't feel equipped and 5 being people feel fully equipped)

Have the small groups reassemble and feedback to the whole group. Allow feedback and questions of clarification. If there is a lack of clarity about the mission and goals you can then go on to ask the small groups to consider the following questions.

> **The blockages – 30 minutes**

- What things are standing in the way of everyone understanding and signing up to our mission and goals?
- What things are preventing us from properly equipping our people to fulfil the mission and goals?
- Are there other things which we are focused on which seem more valuable to us than the mission and goals? (you might suggest a few to get the thinking going on this)
- What are these things and why do we think we value them so highly?

Again have the small groups feedback on these to the main group and allow for questions and discussions.

You're now well placed to get on with the fun part—i.e. answer the question of *how do we keep the things which we value (will probably include strong relationships) and want to focus on whilst at the same time ensuring that the core mission and goals of the organisation are front and centre in everyone's mind? How do we also ensure that everyone understands how they can help to fulfil this mission and these goals?*

You may want to start addressing this with your focus group or you may want to take this away for wider consultation or work on it with the leadership team. Either way you're now ready to get into really enhancing your organisation's effectiveness.

Story:

As we have discussed, our focus on relationships can mean we end up being too nice and, crucially, taking longer than we should to address issues with people.

A senior pastor of a growing church hired a business manager to run the day-to-day operations of that church whilst he maintained an overview of activities and focused on the ministry and pastoral issues. The business manager role had not previously existed, as the size of the church had not warranted this. The pastor's predecessor had employed a secretary, but it was felt that the role should now become a managerial one.

The role was not easy to fill and after a series of unsuccessful interviews a lady from the congregation stepped forward to be considered. She had a business background and strong project management and financial skills. She was a skilled and able individual contributor, but what she was not (as it turned out) was a person who was able to manage and motivate a team, especially a team containing volunteers. The church continued to grow and pretty soon, in order to be effective, this lady had to harness the energy and enthusiasm of the team and to give direction to both volunteers and staff members.

This new need to manage others left the business manager feeling overwhelmed and pretty soon she began to communicate this to those who were dealing with her. Staff members heard time and time again that their requests were creating too much hassle and the lady became short tempered and grumpy with those around her. This negative approach grew to such an extent that people started to avoid her and the effectiveness of the organisation started to suffer. Things came to a head when the senior pastor took some study leave, on his return he found the manger and staff at loggerheads and, in his words, things had reached 'explosion point.'

It had been clear for some time that the lady in question was not the right fit for the job. Indeed the pastor and she had been talking about this for a period of *three years*. These were years in which the church was growing from 800 to about 1200, and where the staff team was growing from a dozen to twice that number. In short, the job was proving to be too big for her just at the time when the church really needed effective administrative management to ease it through this growth phase.

The elders of the church became engaged in the issue and together with the pastor and they worked with the lady until she saw that she could not carry on in the job and she resigned. This was not a simple decision as although this person was enduring some pain in the role, she also felt that the church was like her family, and despite the pain she was reluctant to give up the contact she had with this group. Thankfully, the work done by all parties meant that, although she resigned, there was not a breach in relationships and she continued to attend the church and be a member of its congregation. Reflecting on all this the senior pastor drew two key lessons.

Firstly, more should have been done up front to check if this person was a fit for the role. If this had been done it might well have become clear that she was an effective operator when she undertook tasks on her own, but that she was not equipped to manage and motivate others. The pastor now signs up to the old adage of HR managers, 'if in doubt don't hire.' When a role is proving tricky to fill it is often very tempting to reach out and fill it with someone who's available, even when you feel in your heart of hearts that they are not quite right for the job. You rationalise that they will grow into the job and that over time all will be well. Unfortunately in reality the reverse normally happens! Also, remember that if you put the wrong person into a role then you end up not only being unfair to your organisation, but also to this person. You may put them in a situation where they will fail, when they might easily be successful in the right role.

The second piece of learning the pastor draws is that it took too long to address this issue. It seems fairly common in Christian bodies that we do take a long time to address performance issues. This is often because we are very gradually trying to work the issue through with the person or people concerned. We want to try and ensure that as little hurt as possible is caused. This is a laudable intention, however you have to balance this against the needs of the organisation. Is a whole bunch of suffering taking place in the body and are relationships being soured because the issue is not being addressed speedily enough? It might well be that both the person concerned and the rest of the organisation would benefit more if the problem is addressed more quickly and clearly as soon as it becomes apparent. Another thing that addressing an issue early might do is give you a greater number of options as it can mean that positions are less entrenched than if it drags on longer, which in turn might mean that other solutions, for example getting someone to move to another role, might be open to you.

CHAPTER 3

Agendas and Alignment

Multiple agendas

CONSIDER FOR A moment that we are the crew of a rowing boat. If we all decided to row in different directions the likelihood is that the boat would not move at all. If it does move it certainly won't be forward in a straight line. In this case, if we all decide that the best way to resolve the problem is to simply row harder in our own direction, then we're likely to make matters worse, not better!

We see something like this phenomenon in Christian as well as in other organisations. People within the organisation have multiple and often conflicting agendas that they work on, either as individuals or sub-groups. The effect of this is a lack of alignment, which means the organisation as a whole does not line up to achieve its mission and goals. This is costly in terms of time and effectiveness. Indeed things can get worse than this. Multiple agendas can have an even more negative consequence, especially if they lead to turf wars, rivalries, and the deterioration of the coherence of the body as a whole.

Set against this, it seems to be true that really great organisations have a very high degree of clarity as to what they are about, and what they are trying to do. In other words they have a clear vision. They work hard to ensure this vision is signed up to by their membership, and they then do *a few things* extraordinarily well in support of this vision. They generally don't try to do everything and cover every base as they recognise that this will dissipate their effectiveness. This clarity of purpose and focus is demonstrated by Paul when he says, 'I am bringing all my energies to bear on this one thing, forgetting what is behind and looking forward to what lies ahead' (Phil. 3:13).

Passion soaked agendas

We all know that this challenge of multiple agendas is not unique to Christian organisations!

I am sure many of us have seen people pushing their own agendas in secular work. We may even have seen this in some family situations and even in our friendships. Human beings often want to achieve what they regard as the best outcome and are prepared to position things to achieve this 'desired' end.

So are Christian organisations any different in this regard? Well I think that there is a difference, and ironically this can make the issue of multiple agendas a far greater issue for us than it is in the secular world!

The multiple agenda issue seems to take on a special form in Christian bodies, and possibly other organisations that have a large volunteer base. I would express this special form in the following way; many people in these organisations are not there for the money, their pay is probably less than they would make in the commercial world, or they are volunteers. They are therefore driven by motives other than financial reward, and one of these motives is significance, i.e. gaining significance in their own lives. This can be a very good and healthy thing but it can mean that people become highly wedded to what they are doing in an organisation, and develop a high sense of ownership of 'their area.' The issue of what they are doing can become very personal and very significant to them, even part of their view of who they are as a person.

Their activity, therefore, can come to be more important to them than what the organisation as a whole is trying to do and they can also come to believe that no one else, not even the head of the organisation, can or should tell them how to run their activity. They don't perceive that anyone else has the right to interfere as they often believe at some deep level that they have given a sacrificial amount in terms of material and time to make their project work. They feel that the leadership's role is merely to tell them that they are doing a great job and to provide additional resources if needed. Given this, the leadership clearly face a tough challenge if they what to change or close down this activity!

The person who does the flowers on a Sunday, owns this, they see it as key to the effectiveness of the service, they believe that people appreciate the flowers immensely and they therefore will not take any suggestions on less, different or no flowers kindly!

The multiple agenda issue can become even more 'turbo-charged' by passion. Normally people are not only deriving significance from what they are doing they also passionately believe they are doing *the right thing*. Let's take the case of two church members, Bill and Robert, who believed their church should play two very different roles.

Bill believes passionately that the role of the church is evangelism. He believes it should devote the majority of its time and resources to reaching out to the local community and specifically to reaching the un-churched.

Robert, on the other hand, believes that the time, effort and talents of the church should go into sustaining and deepening its existing community. Really it should be about growth and discipleship and building an exemplary community. He is not against people joining the church but thinks this will happen as the result of having a great community, and this is where the effort should go.

Both believe they are trying to do the right thing. Neither has negative motives, and in fact they both want 'what's best' for their church. Given this, they are convinced that they are right. This conviction of being right leads them to fight their corner passionately for what they believe in.

The problem is that in time this creates real difficulties for their community. To do both things well diverts resources, meaning that neither route can be fully embraced. Two groups develop around the two ideas with Bill and Robert as their leaders. Both sides see the other as standing in the way of real progress and tension builds between the two parties. Much emotion and energy becomes channelled into this dispute. As a consequence this energy is drained from the other things the church should be doing. The dispute drags on until both parties are finally so exhausted that a kind of compromise (which does not really satisfy anyone) is reached.

Now in the secular world people can be very passionate about their agendas. However normally such conflicts are resolved more quickly as the needs of the organisation are clear, and the boss will eventually makes a choice which all are expected to follow.

We have to be careful as Christians that our work and ministries do not become more about ourselves, and our needs, than the needs of the organisation and family which we are serving. St Augustine defined sin as loving in the wrong order. If we love money more than our families then we have got our priorities wrong and have put out trust and security in something that will disappoint. Equally if we value our families, spouses and children, more than we love God the same will apply. This does not mean we should not love our families, of course we should, but we should not love them more than God. Similarly we have to be careful we don't fall in love with what we do and make it completely central to our lives. If so, we might well end up worshipping this, making it our idol, and being 'closed' to the wider needs of our organisation and the other people in it.

Calling

During the interviews for this book, many of the interviewees talked about 'calling' and the challenge this could present. This is where people feel called by God to undertake a particular ministry, initiative or venture. They not only feel called but normally feel theological justified in what they are doing.

Like the passion soaked agenda, this means people will hold tightly to their ideas, beliefs and perceived mission. In this circumstance they and their leadership may feel that no earthly authority can challenge this calling, even if it does not fit with the organisation's vision and plans *or even if it is counter to these*. Often, in these circumstances, people are able to quote a piece of scripture which justifies what they are doing. This makes them feel that all other inputs and challenges are irrelevant or just plain lacking in faith.

Calling can of course be a wonderful gift and one that we should all acknowledge and be grateful for. Of course calling is not itself a reason why Christian organisations struggle with the people side of things. It is more that unchallenged calling, lacking in validation, can be an issue. Calling seems to become an issue when the leadership does not feel equipped to address it fully and well. Part of this means working through a person's calling so it is honoured but also properly tested. One way of doing this is may be to ask them to take some small steps to see if this is God's direction or their own imagination.

In addition to this we have to accept that not every calling can or should be carried out in every organisation. It may well be that a person has a deep and real calling but that this does not fit with their current organisation's focus. In this case it is legitimate to expect this calling to be carried out in another body that is aligned and focused on the area the person feels called to serve in. Effective organisations cannot and should not focus on everything, so on occasions the individual will need to find a new place to operate from rather than expecting their current body to change its focus and direction.

Theological alignment

All of this talk of multiple agendas and lack of alignment is fine you might say, but misses the most fundamental alignment challenge which Christian organisations face. That is a lack of *theological* alignment.

This is an area that the secular world does not face and is an area of huge passion. It's a place where, because it is related to faith, ideas and positions it can not easily be moved to accommodate a single view or single direction. It is not unheard of for members of the same body to hold different beliefs with regard to key theological issues. Hours of debate can and are spent on huge issues such as the primacy of scripture, the virgin birth, and even the resurrection.

There is (rightly) real passion in theology and so there is a very real opportunity for division to take place and for mischief to be done. This is a complex issue demanding much scholarship. I am not going to attempt to unpack it fully in this book as this is designed to be a helpful handbook with regard to people issues in Christian organisations. However, I would offer a few thoughts which I hope are helpful and which have been introduced and underlined by my interviewees.

Theologically, an organisation needs to stand somewhere, it can not say it has no view and just be all things to all people. If it does this, then this lack of grounding is likely to cause problems in the future, problems such as future disagreements and the inability to generate long-term success, as the foundations are not deeply rooted.

Having said this, the organisation also needs to decide what is doctrinally core, and where it is 'happy' to see a range of views expressed. In this regard a Christian organisation might well see the resurrection as a core belief—in fact many of us would say that without this Christianity lacks the power and relevance that we believe it has. However it might also hold no particular view on male-headship, or the 'qualifications' required to receive communion, or the dress-code which needs to be adopted.

What seems to matter here is that the core beliefs are understood, adhered to and used as a key part of the alignment of the organisation. This allows the organisation's members, both paid staff and volunteers, to 'buy into' these beliefs, and know what they are supporting. It also enables those who are unable to support the theological direction of the organisation to find a home elsewhere.

Staying the course

So, getting agendas that point in the same direction and achieving alignment looks to be something that Christian organisations need to prioritise.

Not only do we need to do this but we also need to consistently apply this direction and alignment, or we may give ourselves problems over time.

One of my interviewees said this challenge was a little like building a house on solid foundations but then adding an extension built on sand!

Organisations can start out well, but then lose focus. Funnily enough this lack of focus can be caused by success. Rapid growth can mean the original core team are supplemented by many newcomers wanting to try new and different things. It can also be generated by the enthusiastic leader who has a solid vision at the beginning but as growth comes he or she decides that the organisation can now try to do a whole raft of unrelated activities.

Defining success

When seeking to embrace a common goal and vision and to be aligned to this goal, Christian organisations may face another unique challenge.

This is that people may have very different views of what *success* looks like and what the body should be trying to achieve. In this circumstance it is difficult to achieve real alignment which people buy into with their heads and their hearts, and it is easy for this debate to run and run within the organisation.

Businesses normally define success in a fairly straightforward way, although they may have lots of *add-ons* to the core objective. In the base case their success is normally about profitability, growth, and increasing shareholder value. These objectives may lead to discussion about how to do this; should we be a premium player, a discounter, the biggest in the field, the number one competitor, should we be national or international—but the basic aim is normally clear.

In a Christian organisation agreeing this fundamental goal can prove a lot more challenging! Let's take a few moments to look at a couple of aspects of this.

In a Christian context we are called to be faithful in this generation and the next. This can lead to some saying we can't judge if we're successful because even if it looks like we're failing now, in time our faithful service will pay off.

You sometimes see this argument deployed where a church is not growing, or a particular ministry is not flourishing. In these circumstances the idea is advanced that it does not matter that numbers never exceed a handful because in the long run this work will be significant and cannot be judged now. This rationale continues to be applied even when this small group are exhausted and are clearly driving themselves into the ground. It is often derived from not agreeing what success looks like at the outset, setting the goals clearly and all signing up to these. Without this it's hard to argue against the idea that one day this faithfulness will be rewarded.

Another challenge that you hear to the idea of success is people saying 'it's how we are that matters, not what we do.'

This means if we're serving, loving, believing, prayerful and holy in our attitudes then this is success in itself and does not need to be supplemented by what we achieve. In fact we're saved by grace and not by works, so let's not get too hung up on growing our organisations, or raising additional resources and devoting them to new ministries. Let's not worry about trying to reach new geographies because ultimately it's not a numbers game.

This challenge obviously has truth in it. However this looks a little like a half- truth. Clearly how we are and the state of our faith is vital, but it is a starting point. We are also called to use all of our energy and skills as effectively as we can. In the parable of the talents the three servants are called to take and use their talents and to multiply their effect. In Colossians 3:23—24 we are called work well, not poorly, and so do the best we can.

Rick Warren's *The Purpose Driven Church* contains a section on myths about growing churches and says that some believe that God only expects us to be faithful. Warren counters this by saying this is only half true. As well as being faithful God also expects us to be fruitful. This fruitfulness is defined as practising the truth, winning unbelievers to Christ, and repentance. He explains that we are expected to bear fruit, 'you did not chose me, but I chose you and appointed you to go and bear fruit—fruit that will last' (John15:16) and, 'we pray this in order that you may live a life worthy of the Lord and may please him in every way: bearing fruit in every good work,' (Col 1:10). Again, we are not expected to be wholly passive but are required to use the abilities we have been given in kingdom building work.

This argument about success can be taken further by some with the refrain that, 'God will provide'. Success is for Him and not for us, so we do not need to struggle with this. Indeed we should not struggle but just, 'wait upon the Lord'. All of this is true but again not the entire picture.

God has done the most amazing things in my life in spite of me, never mind through my own efforts. These things have included unlocking seemingly intractable problems at home and work, blessing my wife with the job she wanted after an absence of four years from the work place, unlocking my dyslexic son's real abilities, blessing major projects I have been involved in, and providing me with opportunities which I could not have imagined to be possible. I have also been protected in times of high vulnerability and helped to make major changes when this was right.

However this does not mean that I believe that I should not use the common sense and gifts that God has given me. I see it this way; 'we must always remain very open to God's leading and seek His help—but we must also try to do the best we humanly can.' If we're off track, He'll bring us back on track, and if what we are trying to achieve is right in His eyes but is beyond us, He will help us. However this does not mean we should sit back and wait for God to shower everything upon us. Whilst we should actively pray and seek God's will, we must also be prepared to use our own talents and initiative to move things along, to embark on initiatives, and to seek the outcomes that seem right.

This reminds me of the old joke where a man kept praying to God to win the lottery. Each week he's disappointed, but prays some more. More disappointment, eventually his prayers become a little frustrated, and he starts to accuse God of not helping. Eventually a voice from heaven calls out to him 'Joe—if you want to win the lottery, then at least buy a ticket!'

More seriously, if we don't use the gifts God has given us then it will be hard to get to heaven and say, as Paul hoped to, that we have been good and faithful servants.

What does all this mean for me?

Again, as we did in chapter 2, let's take a look at an analytical tool that may help you to judge if you have an issue with alignment in your organisation, and if multiple agendas are at play.

Analytical tool:

If you want to see if your organisation is aligned behind common goals or if multiple agendas exist you might want to have a cross sections of people complete a short questionnaire that you can then analyse. The key in this is to ask them what's important to them and then see if this is consistent with the mission and goals of the organisation.

This might look something like this:

Individual's agenda
1. What do you believe the mission of our organisation should be?
2. What should be our goals for the coming year?
3. What are you most committed to delivering within the organisation?
4. How does this fit with the mission and goals you outlined above?

How well are they being motivated by by the vision and goals
5. What are we currently doing that you would want to see us stop doing?
6. Do you feel part of the organisation's decision making?—scale 1 to 5, 1 not at all and 5 very much
7. Do you know what is expected of you by the organisation?—scale 1 to 5, 1 not at all and 5 very much
8. Does the organisation communicate its objectives well?—scale 1 to 5, 1 not at all and 5 very much
9. Do you feel you opinions count?—scale 1 to 5, 1 not at all and 5 very much
10. How motivated are you by the organisation's mission and current gaols?—scale 1 to 5, 1 not at all and 5 very much

If you're getting back a whole range of ideas in answer to questions 1 to 5, the likelihood is that there is no real alignment around vision and goals, and if the answers in 6 to 10 are in the low range then its likely that there is little buy-in to what the organisation is trying to do. Together, these will give a clear flag that changes need to be made—see chapter 16 on getting aligned.

Story:

In terms of alignment, I offer this story to illustrate where this was an issue. The story concerns churchmanship, an issue which many of you will be familiar with. It's an Anglican story and as many will know the Anglican Church is a broad church, containing as it does many differing ideas and practices. In this story an Anglo-Catholic Minister takes up office in an Evangelical diocese. Part of this process entailed the Minister agreeing to not promote a different type of churchmanship to that which was predominant in the diocese.

The Minister appears to have agreed to this provision and starts work. Very soon, the Bishop is made aware by concerned members of the congregation that some clearly Anglo-Catholic practices are taking place. Principally, and possibly predictably, these were taking place during communion. The Minister had instituted a practice where the Host (the bread) was walked around the church for adoration. It was not then taken by the congregation but rather was adored as the Body of Christ. As many of you will know this is at odds with the Evangelical teaching that the last supper is an act of remembrance, and that this remembrance is done by people taking part in the supper i.e. eating the bread and drinking the wine. Evangelicals do not believe that the bread and wine is transubstantiated into the body and blood of Christ, they believe that they remain bread and wine and that this is a ceremony of remembrance where those present should take part in the supper.

In this instance there was a clear lack of alignment between the individual and the diocese. Moreover, this alignment fell on the most difficult of territories, namely differing theological approaches and beliefs. The Bishop was now faced with the choice of either ignoring the issue or acting, and in this case it was no choice at all as not acting could not be contemplated.

Many discussions now ensued between Bishop and Priest. The Priest said his acceptance by the parish had shown that he would continue to uphold the traditions he had always practised, he had expected the diocese to see this in his acceptance letter and when they failed to challenge him on it, he felt that he was able to pursue what he thought was right. The Bishop clearly disagreed saying that the traditions and practices of the diocese were clearly understood and widely know amongst the Anglican community.

A dialogue carried on and during this both men developed a healthy respect for each other. They focused on the issue not on personalities and they had a number of 'straight discussions.' The issue was not resolved in a day, it took time, but the Bishop knew that he had to get alignment on this practice—that is he could not allow it to continue and a way forward had to be found. This way forward did not include the Bishop simply being able to move or suspend the Priest because in this diocese the tenure of the Minister was firmly established and the suspension of his licence would have required a long, protracted debate.

In the end a compromise was reached and the practice was 'suspended' indefinitely. Both men continue to work together and have a good relationship. The story shows that the alignment issue had to be addressed, it was not quick or easy to do, but eventually a way forward was found. Failure to address the issue would have struck at the very foundations of the diocese's practice and beliefs; if this practice had not been addressed, the evangelical nature of the diocese and what it stood for would have been at risk.

The issue was not swept under the carpet and avoided and by focusing on the issue and not on personalities a good working relationship remained at the end of this process.

CHAPTER 4

Human Leaders and Human Followers

Human leaders

It seems that you can't pick up a book on organisations and their transformations today without being led to the conclusion that leadership is the all-important factor. It is often portrayed as the 'silver bullet' from which all success or failure flows. In short, leadership has become a very sexy subject. We are all captivated by the idea that a person or a small group of people can set or change the destiny of a major institution or enterprise. These figures have gained real prominence in our world and we all have our own heroes and villains.

We now need to ask if it is also true in the Christian world that the type and quality of our leaders determines the success of our organisations? More specifically, does it contribute to the struggle we seem to have with the people side of things?

The answer to both of these questions seems to be 'yes, of course, leadership plays a key role.' It is not the only factor, but it is very significant. Moreover, in the Christian world there appear to be some specific leadership challenges which we see less often in secular society. These challenges seem to highlight some of the reasons we have specific people management challenges.

Equipping and experience

Leadership, and more specifically management, skills are things we have not always valued in Christian organisations. Many of the interviewees for this book felt that this was often demonstrated in our seminaries. Here, many felt that future pastors, ministers and priests were often not prepared for leadership roles, and indeed this activity did not seem to be highly valued.

The seminaries were seen as (rightly) valuing academic study and bible knowledge. There was agreement that they also valued oratory, vision casting, teaching, pastoring and preaching. However, leadership and managerial skills seemed to get much less coverage. As a consequence, many were not surprised that young pastors often did not appreciate that they might well be called upon to lead and manage complex organisations.

These new pastors may also not appreciate that this leading and managing might mean that they would have to build a plan to turn their vision into reality. That they will have to institute great hiring practices, put in place performance management, ensure effective money management and delegate using good empowerment techniques. Sometimes, not only did they not appreciate that they would be called upon to do many of these things, but often they didn't even know they existed, *and were not sure that this is what they wanted to do in any case.*

Now, clearly this is not universally the case in all Christian organisations.

Indeed, in most sizeable ones their leaders have extensive leadership and managerial experience and have 'signed up' for this part of the job.

Nevertheless, there does seem to be a challenge for us and this challenge is ensuring we are effectively equipping Christian leaders to lead. It might be that we're not being fair to future Christian leaders because we are not equipping them better to lead and helping them understand what this means.

Contrast this to the commercial world. If we take any good company then we know that they will not allow someone to manage a business without spending years grooming them. They will test them in a series of roles and situations before they become MD, president, or general manager. Of course, they recognise that there are natural leaders and managers. However, they also recognise that even these people will find it hard to be successful without great preparation and training.

A less deferential world

So equipping through leadership and managerial training might well be something that we need to do more.

In addition, it also seems true that world has become steadily less deferential over the last 50 years or so. We are less used to giving automatic respect to societal leaders, our politicians, for example, have certainly not enjoyed this respect for a number of years! However, this trend has moved beyond politicians to doctors, judges, teachers, priests, bankers and media figures.

At the same time as deference for our leaders has decreased, our expectations of them have risen. We know that many of the volunteers in Christian organisations, both charities and churches, are highly qualified and skilled people. Outside their voluntary work they are holding down significant jobs, and they expect their Christian leaders to be as good as they are at running the organisation. Well maybe not as good as they are (*some of these people have pretty good opinions of themselves*) but they do expect that they will know how to harness the talents of others, and how to compensate for any weaknesses that they may have.

This combination of decreasing deference and increasing expectation means that Christian leaders today have to come to their roles with real training and capability to lead their organisations. Without this they are likely to make their potential supporters frustrated by their limitations, and the impact these limitations have on the organisation.

Longevity

In the Christian world we can see many examples of leadership longevity.

This can be a great thing. I will argue elsewhere that the voluntary nature of many Christian organisations means that it takes time to enact change—you have to get everyone on board, or at least a critical mass of people, to make sustained changes; longevity in office allows time for this kind of consensus building to happen. It can also mean consistency is promoted, which can give strength and a clear sense of purpose to an organisation, be it Christian or secular.

However, in the Christian and not for profit worlds, it's not unheard of for the same leader to stay in place for many years. Often this person is the founder of the organisation. This person's vision and passion may well have made the organisation a reality and because of this they enjoy an unassailable position pretty much forever. This can create its own problems. For example, the visionary leader who did a great job getting the idea off the ground and enthusing everyone may not be the person to run the organisation once it has grown to a size where it can't be run informally by one person. Without becoming a bureaucracy, it will probably need new systems, structure and processes to move ahead and thrive.

None of this means the founder did a poor job but it may mean that someone with different talents and a different profile is now needed to lead the organisation in this second phase. This can be hard for the founder to recognise, and so some critical years are lost before this need becomes so obvious that a change is brought about.

This can be exacerbated because in the past Christian and charity leaders have often ascended to their roles because of time served. They were attracted to the mission of the organisation because of their hearts, not because they wanted a managerial role or because they had the skills to do it. So they ascend to a role where they not only lack skills but also lack the motivation to do the role—they want to serve the mission not run the organisation.

I raise this issue as it was raised with me by a number of people—it's a 'watch out' in running effective organisations. Clearly, at different phases, an organisation may need a different kind of leader and sometimes it takes great humility to be able to recognise and implement this.

Blind spots

Extraordinary as it may sound, even in the larger Christian organisations, some Christian leaders can have blind spots!

What do I mean by this outrageous suggestion, you may ask?!

Simply this, many people who get to the top of Christian organisations can get there as a result of their gifts as a teacher, or speaker, their charisma, and their ability to cast compelling visions. They have reached the top without experiencing or needing good leadership, much less good managerial practices and systems like job clarity, performance management, team building, effective hiring practices, and people development. As this was not their route to 'success', they may see no need for these processes in their organisation, or indeed may not even be aware of them.

Let's consider a fictional character, Bishop Bob. Bob is recognised as a towering intellect, a preeminent scholar and a speaker who can hold an audience in the palm of his hand. He also has great personal charisma and charm. This powerful combination of factors has moved him swiftly and fairly effortlessly through the hierarchy. Following ordination he served a short time as a curate, soon was given his own parish, spent some time working with the Archbishop, was given a teaching post and became a Bishop in his forties.

Bob is a very able person, but he does what we all do, he reacts to the world through who he is and his own past experience. At his core he really believes leadership means charisma, brainpower, the ability to teach—and not much more. He really is not interested in 'good managerial practices' and in fact finds them faintly boring.

He does not see the need for processes that could develop others and sustain the organisation over the long term. He prefers rather to believe that people should rise as he did, through teaching, academic brilliance, and personal charisma. Given this outlook he transmits this view in his dioceses and appoints people who fit with his model.

None of this means he is a bad person—he merely has some decided blind spots that he has little understanding of and no motivation to address.

The likelihood of him addressing people issues and developing people is further reduced by the fact that these things are not what are expected of him. He is not really expected to spend a huge amount of time developing and coaching his priests. Instead he is expected to contribute his academic ability to church debates, to spend much time interacting with his peers, and to being a significant teacher.

Given this combination of factors, it can be hard to have a leadership that dedicates itself to raising-up leaders who will be instrumental in growing and nurturing effective local organisations.

Another aspect of this blind spot can also be temperament.

There seem to be some Christian leaders who, whilst they are quite brilliant teachers and inspirational speakers, are not so good relating to the ordinary man or woman in their midst. There can be a certain lack of that wonderful quality Christ had to be consistent and engaged no matter who he was relating to and to have a message (often personal) for them all.

Christian leaders need to ensure that they don't become 'legends in their own lunchtime' or fall prey to the 'celebrity trap' that can allow humility to fly out of the window. Sometimes leaders can believe their own publicity, e.g. that they are valued for their inspirational nature and don't need to come down to earth to deal with people on a more personal and practical basis. This situation can be made even more difficult because in Christian circles we don't always promote feedback and development of self-awareness as things we expect our leaders to embrace.

Building teams

Nothing really effective is achieved in human terms unless it's achieved by a team. Having said this, building effective teams and working through others can be something that some Christian leaders find hard to do. This is critical because normally the leader is responsible for building the team. He or she must be capable of selecting and motivating the talent to fill the team. If not, then it's unlikely that a great team will fall into place.

Leaders may not have the talent to form teams and they may also feel other constraints in this regard. As well as not knowing how to harness the talents and ability of others, leaders can also feel that everyone expects them to do all things, and complete all work. They can also feel that it takes 'too long to delegate'. They may feel that if they delegate it will be done less well than they could do it themselves—by the way when you first delegate this is nearly always true.

In addition to this, if the organisation lacks some of the basic tools like clear objectives, role clarity, measurement and performance management, then it can be hard to set up an effective team, and hard to sustain and utilise it.

The Christian leader, in order to build a team or work through others, needs to be a phenomenal communicator, not only from the front of a room, but also in small groups and one to one. Not only do they need to be great at this, they have to expect it to take a great deal of their time. Not all Christian leaders have the ability or inclination for this continual communication and as such they are unlikely to motivate and engage others or get people to support the vision of the organisation. There is a huge communication piece in being the leader of any organisation, especially one that has many volunteers, and there is also a need for consistency in the message.

People need to hear things many times through many different media to ensure they fully register them. Don't expect that one talk from the front will ensure that all people have heard and signed up to a new initiative, the opposite is likely to be true.

I also wonder, when meeting Christian leaders, if there is not something else going on, at a psychological level, which sometimes makes it difficult for them to form and develop teams. It seems that as well as some lack of training and skills in team formation, some Christian leaders can have a specific view of their own authority and how it should be exercised. They can appear to believe that they have a unique kind of authority which means that they should be in control of every issue and that others should naturally defer to them and accept their wisdom in all matters. If this view is held, it becomes difficult to build real teams as other people are not given real empowerment to fulfil their part and real encouragement and support to take on responsibility. In fact the leader keeps hanging on to all the real decision-making.

One example of this is where, after a lot of encouragement (pushing), the leader agreed to involve the wider-leadership in defining where the church went next with its youth work. This area was a critical pillar of the church's work, vital to encouraging young people and new families to join the church. The pastor invited other people to contribute to the thinking on this area, and in his own mind he believed he reached out to others in the leadership for their ideas. However, even after one meeting, it became apparent that he had decided the way forward on this issue, who would be invited to lead in this area and what their brief would be. Whilst genuinely believing he was consulting and involving, the reality was he wanted to control this issue fully and had made up his mind what would happen in this area. This was in line with his normal behaviour and only served to reinforce people's view of his leadership. It also meant people gave up trying to help as they felt that their views were not valued. Funnily enough, the individual concerned didn't seem to realise that he behaved this way and genuinely thought he'd tried to consult and involve others on this matter.

Vulnerability

When I set out on this book I had no idea that vulnerability would be so often referred to as a factor affecting Christian leaders. Many Christian leaders feel pretty vulnerable in their communities.

Some of this is for the obvious reason that they 'enjoy' their tenure from a congregation or laity who can turn them out if they are not happy with what they are doing. Also, at a more fundamental level, we have to accept that Christian communities can sometimes be judgemental and difficult places to operate. Clearly this is not universally true, but we all need to pause and reflect on our own circumstance and if we're making it tough for our leader—I'm sure I've done this in the past.

Christian leaders often operate in an environment where people are not afraid of voicing their views. This normally covers all subjects and is often via email when they are still in a state of high dudgeon. This high dudgeon might be about the music at a service, what was said in the sermon, the latest stewardship drive or one of a hundred other possible issues. Strangely enough, people feel that they can direct a level of rudeness to their pastor that they would not dream of applying to anyone else outside of a bar fight.

In addition to this, many Christian leaders (and their flock) feel that they must exhibit superhuman standards at all times. They are constantly being scrutinised and their work is often a 'whole life' matter. There is no real division between home and work—they are always on call for all needs. Christian work is often a full life commitment, and its leaders cannot go home at the end of the day and close the door on their job. Often their relationship with their communities is often one of 'family' and this family can expect to call on them at any time and they always need to be able to respond and to respond in a giving, supportive and helpful way. This is a heavy demand and the need to always be in the right place emotionally to cope with the family's needs creates demand and vulnerability—any slip up may not easily be forgiven or forgotten.

Added to this, we have high expectations of our leaders not only in terms of standards but also in terms of role capability. We expect that they will be great teachers, great pastors, great leaders and great community builders. It's a lot of expectations to carry! This load can be exacerbated as the leader can have a fear of failure and loss of face. These fears are usually generated because the leader feels that he must project something akin to perfection at all times. This worry can often be much lessened when a person has been through a tough time—maybe even experiencing failure, and learning how to deal with this, and learning to take a more sanguine view of it.

In addition to this, in Christian organisations we tend to have and see many needs. People who become part of a Christian community can bring with them a series of needs; the need for fellowship, the need for recognition, the need for significance, the need to be heard. All of this can increase a leader's vulnerability as everyone expects their need to be met and people tend to be unsettled or even critical if this does not happen. This is hard enough for a leader to achieve, but in addition to this the leader may want the members to focus on something which is not central to them. This can even occur when leaders want to develop discipleship and to ensure people grow in their Christian maturity. This objective, and especially the commitment it requires, may not be the prime objective for the individual. Therefore there is a potential struggle here as the leader tries to promote what he or she feels the organisation needs, whilst the members really want their own needs to be prioritised and met. This struggle can lead the leader to feel unsupported and even undermined.

A leader's sense of vulnerability can lead them to adopt a number of 'strategies' that can add to an organisation's people problems. These strategies include not confronting issues as they feel that if they do they will get hurt in the process. This is a simple avoidance strategy. Unfortunately, it hardly ever works as the difficult issues generally don't go away in fact they normally increase in intensity if they are not addressed.

Another strategy is for the leader to try and deal with all issues and initiatives on a one to one basis to avoid debate in a wider group. This strategy is designed to increase their control of a situation and to minimise the 'danger' of disagreement and confrontation. The problem with this approach is that it is not a great way of empowering and involving a wider group of people and it does not allow for healthy debate which may generate useful ideas. It's an approach that is often designed to try and control the issue and the reactions to it. Having a thin skin and vulnerability can also lead to using control in another way. The leader tries to control all events and decisions so that no one else has the power or opportunity to challenge them and confront them on issues. Again this reduces the riches that an organisation gains from involving many diverse people in its work and growth.

Yet another approach sometimes seen in Christian leaders is that they try and ensure that they only have to deal with their 'own people' in the organisation. That is those who are supportive and like-minded, rather than those who are perceived to be critical and difficult. This approach tends to miss the opportunity and richness gained by bringing detractors and sceptics on board. It may also lead to a continual changing of personnel rather than fully utilising the people already in place. Much is written today about getting the right people on the right seats in the bus i.e. right people in the right position in the organisation. The thinking is that this enables the organisation to flourish.

This is true and it does deliver great leverage, however it does not mean that when a new head comes into an organisation, everyone must be changed. You may inherit people of great talent who merely need to be persuaded of the need for change and who will then deliver great things. Also it may be that people do not need to be shipped out of the organisation but do need to change their role in order that their skills and motivation can be put to best use. Euphemistically we say that the people need to be recalibrated, this tends to be taken as meaning all of them need to be changed—some may, but be careful before you throw out the good along with the obstructive.

Turning now to the followers, rather the than leaders, we should note that if we want to see our organisations run well and experience effective leadership then it may be that we have to find the right way to support our leadership.

I have seen many people do this—they give great feedback highlighting what needs to be addressed but in a way which balances this with the positives. They also do this in a way that shows that they care about the person and genuinely want them to succeed. We all have these types of people in our communities, and it is instructive to look at the model they give us, and to utilise these skills.

As a final word on vulnerability there is an interesting story in Bill Hybels' book *Axiom, Powerful Leadership Proverbs*. In this he tells a story to illustrate that facts are the friend of the leader as they allow for better planning, better decision-making and better monitoring of how an organisation is really doing. All of this is true but this chapter also struck me because of the story he tells. In this story, Bill Hybels was invited to another church to help them take a look at how they were doing and to examine ways forward. He worked with the staff team and told them the day would be in two parts; the morning would be spent evaluating four key areas that can help define success in local churches—evangelism, discipleship, student ministry and compassion initiatives. Then the afternoon would then be spent brainstorming ways to increase effectiveness in each of these areas.

The morning went well and Bill broke the staff team up into small groups and asked them to evaluate how the church was doing in the four areas outlined above. He asked them to rate each area on a one to ten scale, with one being really bad and ten being outstanding. The teams started to work and energy levels and debate soon grew—opinions bounced back and forth and people seemed to be honoured to have been asked for their input. Once all the groups had posted their figures, Bill debriefed the group as a whole. Evangelism scored fours and fives, discipleship got mostly sixes and one seven, student ministry ranked low with all threes, and compassion was at the very bottom of the heap. Bill then did a pre-lunch talk to say that after lunch they'd get on to the fun part, looking at innovative and inspiring ways to raise every one of the numbers—only positive ideas would be accepted. The group left for lunch in high spirits and highly invested in this process. They had been asked to look at where they were and had found this a liberating exercise and were now ready to look at where they could get to next.

The pastor of the church had sat silently all morning and at this point approached Bill to say, 'you can go home now.' Bill Hybels was shocked by this five word bomb shell and asked for clarity. The pastor was adamant; he wanted Bill to go home, right then in the lunch break; there would be no afternoon session. The reason for this—well in the pastor's own words, he had never been so humiliated in all his life. He had found the morning to be a crushing indictment of his ministry. He felt his staff had criticized him and the whole ministry. In no way did he see that this assessment of the church was needed as a prelude to getting the staff energised and aligned on how to move forward.

This kind of reaction has to be borne out of vulnerability, and a real fear of criticism. This pastor would prefer that the issues were not raised, rather than face up to them and have him and his staff team address them together. Clearly there is no way that this form of 'sticking one's head in the ground' will work in the long term. If frustrations are going to go unaddressed, then in time they will boil over and lead to some serious damage. However, it's interesting that vulnerability and a thin-skinned nature can mean that a person would prefer not to look at the issues rather face up to them and take the initiative to do something about them—an initiative which incidentally many would be willing to support.

Issues don't go away if you don't look at them and neither does negative feedback. If you don't have a culture where you're open to feedback then you can be sure it does not disappear, it merely finds another route and goes to another source. Thinking you can avoid what's going on around you is a little like the creature in Douglas Adams' *Hitchhiker's Guide to the Galaxy* who believed that if it couldn't see you then you couldn't see it!

Human followers

As we have seen, Christian leaders have a part to play in our people struggle, but so also can Christian followers.

As Christians we are called to take on an attitude of service and servanthood as modelled by Jesus. We should first seek to serve and then be served. Our own needs should come a distant second to giving to others.

This is the theory, or more accurately the ideal, to which we should strive. However, it seems that there is often a great deal of *personal need* in Christian organisations. People come to the organisation with some very real needs which they are looking to have met. It might be the need for material things, ex-pat churches in the poorer parts of the world attract people and kids who are looking for food, money and other things they lack. In the West these needs might be more emotional. They might take the form of a need for significance, it may be a need for attention, it might be the need to have downtime and have people minister to us, or it might be the need for community. These are powerful and understandable needs, but they can pose some challenges for the organisation.

Firstly, if many have come to receive rather than to give then this can prove a challenge as the helpers are too few for the task. It can mean exhaustion for the leaders as they seek to meet everyone else's needs, and it can mean that there are not enough people who are willing to serve and help the organisation fulfil its mission.

At another level, the expectation that our needs will be met can mean that leaders face criticism because they are not meeting personal needs. They are not being encouraging enough, they don't give enough recognition, they are not making the 'right' things a priority and so on. This criticism can turn to a loss of support and a disengagement of some or all of the membership.

Maybe we need to consider how much we have come to give and how much to take. Sometimes people are in real need and should be encouraged to take all they can, but in many Christian organisations the 80/20 rule applies and seems hard to shift. 20% of the people do 80% of the tasks and give 80% of the money. We know at a theoretical level that it is better to give than receive—sometimes we need to challenge ourselves to put this theory into practice. Normally when we do this we will enjoy real blessings as consequence.

Staff experience

Christian leaders can often inherit their staff teams. In many cases these paid staff have no other experience of work other than working in that organisation or in another Christian body.

A consequence of this can be that when they are asked to meet standards that many in the commercial world would think were very reasonable they look at their leader as if he or she had asked them to fly to Mars. People can come to an organisation with many assumptions. They assume things should be done in a certain way and are often reluctant to change this view.

This lack of professional reference points can make people feel that it is unreasonable to even be asked to turn up to work at a set time, to limit the 'phone calls from home to less than one every hour', and to account for what they do with their time and where they are!

Resistance to these standards seems strange, especially the idea of people accounting for where they are. One of the most basic lessons of ministry is to ensure your colleagues know where you are when you're off-site, and what you're doing. In this way you're going to reduce your own risk of being compromised in some way. Transparency protects against inappropriate and dangerous situations. The pit falls that exist for members of the ministry are great, and experienced leaders know that they and their people need to be on their guard in this respect.

A lack of reference points can mean that the leader can struggle to instil the most basic standards in their team. Normally it is not through 'bloody mindedness' on their part (although this may occur) it is more often from the fact that people don't see the need for these standards, or don't really feel that they should be held accountable for what they do.

They believe (in their own minds) that they are working hard and that should be enough, they should be trusted to get on with their own responsibilities on their own and to their own standards. They may also feel that their standards are God's standards, so no further discussion is required in this area. Perhaps, when we feel this way, we should look again at scripture and see that we are called to aim for excellence and should 'expect to work as if for the Lord', Colossians 3:23.

In Mathew 11:3 John the Baptist's disciples come to Jesus with John's question, 'are you the one who was to come, or should we expect someone else?' John is in prison and it seems doubts are creeping in. Jesus is very clear in his reply. He says John's disciples should return to him and report what they see; 'the blind receive sight, the lame walk, those who have leprosy are cured, the deaf hear, the dead are raised, and the good news is reaching the poor,' Matthew 11:5. Jesus' response here is, 'it's very clear who I am and the good news about me is reaching all people. John is wrong to doubt, he has let go of the standard expected of him.'

This message is reinforced by Jesus' next comment, in Mathew 11:6 he says, 'blessed is the man who does not fall away on account of me.' Here, John the Baptist is reminded of the standards and expectation he must meet. We can see the real power of this passage when later, in Matthew 11:11, Jesus says of John, 'among those born of woman there has not risen anyone greater than John the Baptist.' Here we see that no matter how great a man or woman, they still are required to step up to exacting standards, and to fulfil these standards.

Small staff teams

Many Christian organisations have small staff teams—this is often a function of their size and their funding. This provides a particular challenge as, 'the harvest is plentiful but the workers are few' (Matt 9:37). If this model is going to work, then each staff member has to be dedicated, committed, and very good at their own area of responsibility.

There will always be energy to help train and bring on younger, less experienced individuals, providing that they show the right aptitude and dedication. However, there is not really spare capacity to carry people or allow some staff members to operate in only a few specialised areas that they can master and which appeal to them. In view of this, there is a requirement for hard work and competence in all the people who are on the staff team, and it's also to be hoped that they can turn their hand to many different task when required. This is a demanding specification and unfortunately is not met. This means that these small teams can be overstretched and especially some members of the team can be carrying a disproportionate load whilst others operate on a very limited basis.

What does all this mean for me?

Let's now take a look at an analytical tool that may be helpful in this case. Maybe the most important thing you can address if you're a leader or leadership team is what are your blind spots? Once you know this then you're empowered to start addressing them, and enhancing your own performance and how you deal with others.

Analytical tool:

There are many ways of looking at blind spots and getting feedback to highlight these. An obvious way is to conduct some 360 degree feedback whereby you get feedback from those around you—ideally boss, peers and subordinates. This can be highly effective and can offer some great insights provided that the feedback is genuine, properly collected and analysed. In order to achieve this, the feedback generally needs to be anonymous, as named feedback can end up being very bland. This bland feedback then gives you very little to go on in terms of how you're really perceived and what areas you should address.

However in offering a tool in this section I wanted to offer you an even more telling place to get feedback from than your friends and colleagues—that place is yourself! For this I am grateful to Kate Marshall, a very skilled management consultant, and a practising Christian, who introduced me to the Insights Discovery tool. This tool allows the individual to complete a questionnaire of personal preferences. When analysed, this gives a report to the individual highlighting personal style, including how you interact with others and make decisions.

It talks to your key strength and weaknesses in terms of what you bring to your organisation. It also speaks to the value you bring to a team, how you communicate and also your **possible blind spots**. The tool also offers suggestions for development as well as highlighting what you're going to find easy to do and what will be harder. It outlines what your conscious style is (possibly adopted style for work) and what your natural style is. This enables you to see what you're doing effortlessly and what you're working hard to project to others.

This enormous amount of data comes from a pretty simple questionnaire that you fill in—the normal reaction of people on receiving their report is to be surprised at how much of themselves they can identify!

Such self-generated analysis can give you a whole load of information to go on, but the process becomes even more powerful when you or a team who are working together all undertake this process and are willing to share the results. This not only enables you to consciously commit to tackling some of your blind spots it also enables the team to understand each other so much more. They get a better grasp of why people respond in certain ways, understand that some people like quick interaction and to talk a lot and others need more time to consider issues. Specifically, you will understand people who have opposite styles and preferences to your own and develop some understanding of how to interact with such people. You will also get to see how you're coming across to others—are you being too direct, impatient, or possibly too deliberate and indecisive?

A tool like Insights Discovery, or Myers Briggs or DISC will give you a lot of feedback on how you are and how you're behaving. Then comes the real challenge; are you willing to act on this feedback and possibly share it with others so that they can help you make any changes that might be necessary? Only you can answer this question.

Story:

Continuing with the theme of blind spots, one area this can cause problems is in the appointment of others to key roles. If the leader fails to understand sufficiently the person they are asking to undertake a key role it may well be that problems will occur down the line.

A senior pastor once approached a congregation member who was running a large public organisation to become an elder. The church was expanding and this person had solid experience of governance, a skill the pastor felt would be needed as the church continued to grow. The new elder also had a scientific education and training and therefore brought an eye for detail and for assessing information to the table.

Unfortunately, the combination of a scientific training and working in the public sector for a long time meant the new elder also brought a passion for wanting to consider a lot of detailed information before making a decision. He needed a detailed briefing paper before moving on an issue, and needed to consider a lot of facts. The pastor was a big picture person, used to getting enough information but wanting to move ahead to fulfil the overall vision. He found this need to provide detailed briefings exhausting and frustrating. Moreover, this put pressure and increased workload on a relatively small staff team.

The pastor felt all this demand for information and process was slowing up the church and its ability to respond to situations quickly. He worried that it would ultimately slow the growth of the church.

These two men had not shared enough of their viewpoint at the outset and if they had done so the pastor would have realised that the elder was coming to the role with a conviction. That conviction was that the church's processes were not professional enough, and that more time and energy had to be invested in this area in order to provide the right foundations for the future. The elder, on the other hand, would have understood the pastor's DNA better, that he wanted to do things right but saw the bigger picture as paramount and that excessive detail would drive him crazy. Both were men of conviction with some stubbornness, so their differences on this issue took some time to resolve as each believed that they were doing the right thing and wanted to see this through.

The elder resigned in the end, realising that things were not working out but he stayed in the church and offered to do a role which fitted more easily with the pastor and the leadership team.

The application of this story is that the pastor needed to be more aware of the person he was appointing and more crucially what that person wanted to achieve. His blind spot was to assume he really understood the individual and his motivation before approaching him for the eldership role. If this motivation had been understood at the outset, then a lot of pain, time and frustration might have been saved. This story again ended with everyone 'staying in the boat' but often in such circumstances one of the parties is going to leave and never come back, creating a rift that will be felt long afterwards.

CHAPTER 5

Accountability

Accountability is a clear biblical concept, in Luke 12:48 we're told that if you have received a lot then you will be required to give much back. Moreover, in Luke 19:12-27 the servants are held accountable for what they have done with the mina given to each of them by the rich man. The one who just 'kept it safe' is found wanting and the two who use the gift to good effect and have multiplied it are praised.

However, despite this biblical example, we often don't seem too keen on the concept of accountability when it comes to our own Christian organisations. As one of my interviewees said when talking about accountability, 'we understand the concept, it's the execution we're not good at!' So why do we find this a tough subject and a difficult thing to measure up to?

The 'deal'

It seems that many people join Christian bodies because they believe that a different 'deal' operates in these organisations than in the secular world. This can be summarised as people thinking that they are operating in an environment of grace, and because of this they should not really be judged or held accountable. Moreover, they feel that if they fail to perform then they should be instantly forgiven and the matter should not be talked about, or properly addressed.

This thinking may be even further complicated by the fact that people may feel that because the rewards in a Christian organisation are not financially high, they have traded getting reasonable pay with working in a non-judgemental environment. They expect this environment to be loving, forgiving and infinitely patient. Therefore, they think that part of their deal is to be treated in (what they see as) a very gentle and non-confrontational way at all times. Given this, they don't expect real challenge or to be answerable for what they do.

This thinking can sometimes 'chime in with' the thinking of their leaders. These leaders can be hesitant to ask for accountability, as they are often compassionate people who are conscious of their own shortcomings. They don't want to challenge their brothers and sisters about their shortcomings and performance, the 'splinter in their eyes', as they feel they have to first address the 'plank in their own eye'. This is laudable but again leads us to end up doing the nice thing and not the right thing. Clearly leaders should be humble and aware of their own shortcomings, but this does not mean they should not hold their people accountable and expect that they will deliver what is required of them by the organisation. Jesus had real humility but he was also prepared to set high expectations of others. In Matthew 4:19-22 he calls the disciples and expects that they will follow him without question, giving up their jobs, their homes, and their families to answer his call.

People should be treated with respect but leaders also have obligations to ensure the needs of the organisation are being met. Also, if someone is not positively challenged on their performance we never know if they could grow and do better. Holding people accountable can be healthy for all parties.

Measurement

It's tough to hold people accountable if there is no culture of measurement, and Christian organisations can be poor at measuring. By measurement we mean being able to measure effort and outcomes against a plan. Measurement is a mechanism for quantifying how successful we have been in achieving our objectives.

There seems to be resistance to measurement in many Christian bodies. This can be for a whole number of reasons; sometimes it's due to a distrust of such 'business-like' practices. Sometimes there's a resistance to having people's work calibrated in this way. There can a belief that everything we do is qualitative and cannot be measured in quantitative way. Measurement can be seen somehow as too demanding, or it can be lacking simply because the organisation does not have experience and expertise in this area—that is we don't really know how to do this.

If effective measurement is not applied in either the goal-setting process for an individual or the review process then it can be very hard, almost impossible, to hold someone accountable. This may not always be the case, but the very real danger here is that without measures everything can just be a matter of opinion and viewpoint. Think about conducting a personal review with one of your staff or volunteers. What's likely to happen if you say about an issue, 'I thought this could have been done better.' The likelihood is that the other person will say something like, 'well I thought it was done fine and that's also what all my best buddies have told me too, and by the way what does 'better' mean, I thought it was done well'. I may be overstating this a little but if you have a culture where measurement is not only *not* practised, but is actually distrusted then it's going be hard to hold people accountable for what they have or have not achieved.

Moreover, if there is a culture of not measuring then this culture will subtly communicate itself to the people in the organisation. They will feel that achieving what has been asked of them is not important as the organisation does not measure so is not really expecting them to deliver. Added to this there is an old truism that says 'what gets measured gets done'. There is sometimes little chance to apply this in Christian organisations, so another lever of effectiveness is lost.

I talked in the last chapter about staff experience and reference points. This can again cause a problem in the area of accountability. If it has not been the norm for people to be held accountable for their performance and behaviour, and they have no real awareness that this is standard in many places, then it can be difficult for a new, or existing, leader to institute this culture.

Contrast this approach to measurement with the Saddleback Purpose Statement;

'To bring people to Jesus and *membership* in his family, develop them to Christ-like *maturity*, and equip them for their *ministry* in the church and life *mission* in the world, in order to *magnify* God's name.'

This statement is written in terms of results not activities, and these results are measurable. Indeed Saddleback seeks to measure results in terms of how many were brought to Christ? How many have been equipped and mobilised for ministry and how many are fulfilling their mission in the world? They see this process as really forcing them to evaluate if they are really fulfilling the Great Commandment and Commission.

It's also obviously difficult to introduce a system of measurement, accountability and performance management if the leader is not experienced in or has not been exposed to such systems elsewhere. Normally when you introduce performance management it's an iterative process i.e. you have to do it a few times to get good at it. In view of this, some experience of the process and its benefits can be very helpful in assisting managers to stay the course and get the process in effectively. It is also good to develop some professional systems and processes in this regard, processes that will help all parties.

Measurement and major projects

Another area where measurement and establishing success criteria is important is when you embark on a major project. I was once involved in a church which planted a daughter church. The planters had great enthusiasm and dedication to their cause and the mother church supported the project. However, unfortunately we did not do enough groundwork at the start of the project to agree what the targets would be for the plant, and what the time scale would be for these. We also didn't agree for how long and to what extent the mother church would support the plant, and what success would look like and what we would do if the project was not successful.

Given this the inevitable happened in that the church grew very slowly but the planters saw this as success as faith and fellowship deepened amongst those involved. Meanwhile the mother church wondered if this was not just something which was not successful enough and should be stopped. The lack of a clear agreement, backed by measures at the outset, meant that all this had to be hammered out retrospectively and all these measures and targets had to be agreed once the plant was over 2 years old. The clarity which we should all have had at the beginning was lacking, and although this was later rectified this lack of understanding and agreement cost a lot in terms of time, energy and emotional capital both in the plant and in the mother church.

Who can hold who accountable?

Normally in the secular world it is clear that you will be held accountable for your actions, even if you occupy the most exalted of positions. In a company the CEO must still answer to the board and the board to the shareholder.

However, it is not unheard of in Christian organisations for the leader or leaders to feel that they are not accountable to any person. Their thinking is that they answer to God and that's it. You can see this in some church set ups where the minister believes that they are not answerable to their local laity, and even if they have a bishop they feel that they are only answerable to him for some very specific issues like the form and type of worship and certainly not for performance and effectiveness.

Behind this there often lies history and a particular understanding of the rights and authorities of the pastor. In churches like the Church of England the vicar or rector sometimes owns the freehold to their living—i.e. they cannot be removed, as they actually own the title to their job. As someone once inelegantly put it, these people can't be sacked even if they are found making out with one of the parishioners on top of the piano in full view of the whole congregation! Well maybe in this case they could be let go—but only after a long and protracted legal battle.

In some ways it's not surprising that in such circumstances a person believes they are not answerable to any earthly authority. Added to history there is often a theological or churchmanship view at work here, a view that says being a church leader is not like any other job. This thinking says that church leaders cannot and should not be judged in the same way as other jobs. Indeed only a special few can really understand their role in any case, so most people are ill equipped to judge how the job is being done. My experience is that good leaders, even when they are not formally required to be assessed, do engage in this activity as they value (may not like) being accountable, and the feedback this brings.

Organisations tend to take their tone from the top, 'a fish rots from the head' as a former boss of mine used to say. So, if the pastor will not allow himself to be held accountable, it's highly unlikely that the rest of the body is going to fully embrace this concept.

This can also be made more difficult in that in some organisations it really is not clear who is responsible to whom, and for what. For example, is the pastor responsible to the local lay elders, to the regional leader (or is this person's role only pastoral) or to the bishop in churches that have an episcopate? Often the answer is that no one really knows, so if you don't want to answer for what you are doing then it's normally easy to muddy the water and dodge the accountability.

There is another aspect to the challenge of no one knowing who's answerable to whom and for what. This is that when this is not clear, then individuals or groups may try and fill this vacuum by accumulating power to themselves and seeking to ensure things are done their way. This is not unheard of in churches where a group seeks to control the pastor and the church's agenda. This in turn can lead to resistance the emergence of different factions and the development of turf wars. A whole messy conflict develops which normally sets the church and its mission back, and undermines its effectiveness.

Day to day accountability

Sometimes in Christian originations it can be that an individual's objectives are unclear, not quantified or very long term. This can 'take the pressure off' people to deliver. We sometimes see this in commercial bodies but very rarely in the modern age—competition and cost consciousness are too fierce to allow this to happen. Usually businesses have a very strong focus on profit, which in turn leads to a strong focus on both short and longer term delivery. If a person or team does not fulfil their objectives they normally feel the consequences of this very quickly. Indeed the prevalent culture in a business tends to be one of achievement and this in turn tends to mean that people work hard to deliver as they know that the organisation, their boss and their colleagues expect this of them.

In an environment where there is less expectation of short term delivery and less clarity over a person's actual goals then they may be much less driven by the ever present needs of the organisation. This can be a good thing and can lead to great creativity. However it can also mean people have more time for 'game playing' and politics. This phenomenon is not unheard of in Christian bodies, and unfortunately it is not unheard of for Christian hierarchies, to spend time focused on power politics and ritual rather than on getting to positive outcomes. Great emphasis gets placed on demonstrating who's in charge through elaborate guidelines and process. Focus can be on what people wear, how they follow the liturgy, who's allowed to do what and when. Now some of this has purpose and historical resonance, but often it does not and is part of a process of enforcing the rules for the rules' sake and to show who's in charge. Fulfilling real objectives and real accountability gets lost in amongst the game playing.

Compassion and excellence

Jesus blended real compassion with a demand for excellence. He had compassion for the rich young ruler and because of this he wanted him to put aside what he held most dear (wealth) and to focus instead on God. He had compassion for the woman caught in adultery, and defends her, yet at the end he still sets her a demanding challenge—go and sin no more. He has compassion for the Samarian woman at the well and because of this is prepared to challenge her lifestyle. Yet in spite of this, Christian organisations often seem to believe that compassion cannot be combined with a desire for excellence, i.e. being demanding, setting high standards and holding people accountable. The idea that these things cannot exist in the same space seems to trip us up time and time again.

As a result of this we often don't want to be too demanding or be too clear as to the standards we expect and require, and we certainly don't want to come back at a later date and ask someone how they have done against the task they were set. This is all seen as rather uncomfortable and once again our highly relational culture cuts in. We want to be nice to people so will not ask them to hold themselves accountable, or indeed actually hold them accountable. Again if we look at the bible this looks strange; in Matthew 7:21—23 Jesus makes it clear that people are accountable, saying if you're not real, don't expect to be recognised, and in Luke 6:31 Jesus says that we are expected to treat others as we want to be treated. The bible also makes clear that much (more) will expected of leaders and teachers.

It looks pretty clear that we can have compassion and love people and at the same time seek accountability from them. It looks like our own human desire to be nice and avoid 'confrontation' is getting in the way, rather than any biblical imperative.

A word on nepotism

This is not a subject I had on my radar when I set out to write this book but in interviews people have raised it under the topic of accountability. This is an issue that can have huge consequences if it goes wrong and can be pretty tricky even if it goes right.

Think about a situation where a senior pastor wants his son to follow him into the ministry. The son does this, but does not have his father's talent and ability and it soon becomes clear he should not be kept in his role. His father is then faced with the difficult challenge of firing him. This is challenging enough in normal circumstances but now might involve a family split, with different parts of the family taking different sides. Moreover, father and son relations are unlikely ever to be the same again.

Now imagine how difficult this situation would be for the whole community if the father did not accept the incompetence of the son, he ignored it and would not talk about it. Suddenly the community has a problem now with both the father and the son and the organisation is headed for decline if the issue is ignored or significant pain if the issue is confronted—the rock and hard place choice.

There looks to be a question as to whether healthy and real accountability can exist in these situations. This is made more difficult by the fact that even where the son is a capable person, the rest of the staff and congregation may not be sure if the same standards will be applied to him as to others. They don't know what rules will apply if they disagree with him and want to appeal his decisions to his father.

This does not mean that members of the same family cannot serve in the same ministry. To deny this may mean that the organisation does not use the talents of someone who can contribute a huge amount to the organisation, whilst also growing themselves.

However, it may mean that in this circumstance there has to be even greater transparency and clarity about how accountability works, and especially who is answerable to whom. In such circumstances it might be a good and simple rule to ensure that people who are related do not report to each other. For their sakes, and the sake of the organisation, they need to report and be accountable to a person who is not related to them. Ideally this should be someone who can take an objective view of their performance and contribution.

What does all this mean for me?

The key question here is to understand how we can legitimately create a culture of accountability, and how we can identify if this does not exist.

Analytical tool:

One way you can check if you have accountability in your organisation is to see if the following things are in place. It's very difficult for an organisation to generate a clear sense of accountability if the following are not in place:

1. People are clear who there are accountable to. This not only covers staff but also *crucially* volunteers. It is important that the reporting line is clear and has been spelt out ideally at the beginning of a new job, project or initiative.

2. The organisation has a clear vision and a clear set of priorities. This is likely to take the form of a few things that will be focused on. This clarity may be enhanced by stating what the organisation is *not about* and what it will *not do*.

3. For the staff there are job descriptions and appraisals that align to the vision and priorities and which explain how people can and should play their part. Clearly the effective setting of annual objectives (in the appraisal process) is a cornerstone to making alignment and accountability happen. The organisation should be honest about expectations and how they will be measured.

4. Finally, a culture exists where people have grown up relationships where people are willing to be truthful with one another on an adult-to-adult basis. In this culture people will be authentic and willing to tackle difficult issues.

Story:

In terms of accountability, I heard a rather sad story about accountability being missed. This was not done with any malicious intent and in retrospect the person concerned was mortified at what happened. The point is that we have to keep our need to be accountable at the 'top of mind' at all times and especially when we're heading into difficult situations.

There was a youth worker who began to exasperate her volunteer team because of what they saw as a lack of skill in this area and certainly a lack of skill as a leader and communicator. The pastor agreed that there should be a meeting between the disgruntled volunteers and the youth worker in order to allow people to air the views and hopefully for a new way of working to be agreed.

The meeting took place and the volunteers, some four or five in number, came and were determined that their issues would be clearly heard. Unfortunately, as things progressed, the meeting effectively became a full-blooded attack on the youth worker, and the frustrations which had been building were unleashed. The pastor was at the meeting, and was indeed in the chair. He was accountable for its conduct and for ensuring that all sides were heard and were protected. Somehow this got overlooked in the heat of the meeting and what ensued was a series of negative comments as the youth worker was told how useless she was. The evening assumed an even more negative aspect later, as other people came to hear about the meeting. The view grew that what had happened was unacceptable and most people found it difficult to understand why the pastor had let the process unfold in this way. Tempers began to rise with various people feeling that the pastor should shoulder the blame for what happened and should in fact question whether he could in carry on in his role.

In time fences were mended and apologies given but the youth worker did not feel she could continue in her role and moved on to another church, where she flourished. However, although fences were mended, people remembered what had happened and it clearly weighed in the balance thereafter whenever anything else happened that they were not supportive of—it became a lens through which some people saw the pastor, and it inevitably reduced/damaged his authority despite the fact that people knew him to be a really good man.

Now there may be issues of fairness in all this but the truth of the matter is that the pastor as the leader, and chairman of the meeting, had the main accountability for how this session was conducted. For a moment he forgot this and then paid a heavy price in this regard. Accountability is something that we need to keep in mind, especially if we occupy a leadership role.

CHAPTER 6

Distrusting Professionalism

Quite rational and level headed people in the Christian world can have a high degree of distrust of professionalism and the use of professional techniques. This distrust can be so great that many Christian organisations reject the benefits that a professional approach could bring. These benefits specifically include the effective management of people but professionalism and excellence are often rejected as being 'business' or 'worldly' quantities. In view of this, the reaction to them in Christian circles can be that they are *'not wanted here'*. It is felt that professionalism and excellence are OK if you're Exxon, Walmart, or Marks and Spencer, but they are not things we want in the Christian world. We often see them as meaning being slick, insincere, demanding, and even dull.

More fundamentally, people feel that they show a lack of focus on the Lord and a lack of dependence on Him. The thinking is that we should look to God alone to provide the direction we should take, and to deliver the resources we need. The idea about adopting the wrong focus runs something like this; we want to give glory to God and not to the organisation we have created. As a consequence we get concerned if there is too much focus on the organisation, its processes, and procedures. We (rightly) don't want to become too self-serving, too concerned about how beautiful our organisation and its buildings are and not be focused enough on serving God. This is a reasonable 'watch-out' but not a reason to run a shoddy organisation on the basis that this is somehow God honouring; it's not!

Similarly, we worry about how we can engage in such techniques as strategic planning without being overly dependent on human techniques and forgetting to listen to God, and what He wants us to do. How can we make elaborate financial plans using business techniques (e.g. in fundraising) if we want to be dependant on God and step out in faith and be bold in our spending? How can we define success in human terms, surely this is too limited? All of these are valid challenges but they are only half the picture. Of course we must ultimately be fully dependent on God, but we should also use our God-given talents and human ingenuity to ensure that we do make the best plans possible, use our resources wisely and manage our people effectively.

Valuing amateurism

This distrust of professionalism can sometimes be so profound that we overly value amateurism.

Sometimes it feels like we're like an archer who could easily hit the centre of the target but who prefers to shoot for the outer rings. We do this to show we're not too professional, not too capable, not too business-like, not too showy and not too humanly organised. We end by signing up to the thinking behind the slogan that *'the Ark was built by amateurs and the Titanic by professionals'*!

I would suggest that when we do this we need to be careful that we're not looking too much to our own needs. For example, it sometimes feels very comfortable when our church is like a chaotic family breakfast. We feel it's homely, it's different from work, and it's like a cosy old pullover.

All of this is understandable at one level. Indeed, not all business practices are healthy or right for Christian organisations, and some may go against what we believe and cherish. However, if we are close-minded on this issue we can 'throw out the baby with the bathwater' and lose sight of good business practices that are applicable and helpful in our situation. In many cases good organisational practice is good organisational practice, whether you're a Christian organisation or a commercial one. Having a clear vision, the plans to achieve this, role clarity and a culture where feedback is valued tend to be healthy things regardless of if you're a church or Volkswagon.

The approach of rejecting professionalism and excellence also seems to be out of line with biblical teaching. We can see in Micah that God wanted excellence. He wanted the best sacrifices, not the worst. He wanted excellence and a professional approach not second rate and amateurish standards. Let's be careful we're not engaging in self-indulgence and serving ourselves and not God by rejecting high standards and good practice.

Be selective

There are also times when we reject professionalism simply because it's a closed world to us. Not everyone has a business background, not everyone understands the concepts that others talk about with ease, and certainly not everyone understands the *jargon!*

Those who come from the business world need to be aware of this, and also of the fact that there are many things we don't want to import from this world. It's not certainly unheard of in business that form will be more important that substance. That supporting the latest initiative or fad is more valued that doing the right thing. That focusing on organisation, structure and hierarchy becomes more important than running the business, and that politics is more important than performance. That greed is good. These are the things that give business a bad image. They are also the things that should be left at the door when thinking what to bring into a Christian organisation.

Having said this, there are helpful things; great hiring practices, performance management, sound financial management, clear structures and accountabilities, and clarity of direction and focus. Given all of this, some selectivity is needed, but there are many good aspects of professionalism and business practice. We should not be afraid to apply these things in our Christian organisations. They are tools, which if used properly will help us to operate more effectively and increase the chance of us fulfilling our mission.

Relationships—again!

Once again, our very relational nature can make professionalism a difficult concept for us. This seems to happen at two levels; firstly we may see management as being anti-relational. We often see managerial practices as being harsh, a practice of telling people what to do, we see it like McGregor's theory x manager and not as supportive and challenging in a helpful way. We often forget that good management should be theory y. We forget good managers get the best results through other people and through enabling them to do the very best they can.

Let's take two examples, Bill is a theory x manager and James is theory y. Bill's approach to his people is highly influenced by the assumptions he makes. He thinks people dislike work, and will do all they can to avoid it. He thinks people need discipline. He believes that they can't be trusted and are only motivated by fear and money. He does not think they are creative or loyal, or responsible. Accordingly, he treats them in line with this 'bullying' philosophy. Now, this theory x behaviour is sometimes what we believe management means!

No good modern commercial organisation could survive using this technique, or indeed attract good people. It's more likely they will use James' approach. He thinks people are motivated by achievement. That they are trustworthy, and left to themselves will set higher standards than the boss would set them. He thinks they are responsible, loyal, and a great source of ideas. He treats them accordingly, and as a consequence gets great results from a motivated staff. We can all see that such leadership would be appropriate in any area, secular or Christian.

Secondly, we sometimes resist professionalism and management as we see it as too scientific, and too measurement orientated. We think it's not focused on the values of relationships, forgiveness and love. Clearly a lot depends on how we use management measures and instruments and what our intent is. However, often these kind of scientific measures are used to serve, build and sustain great organisations. In the end they are measures and techniques. They should not be our masters, rather they should be tools we use to achieve what we want. So we should not be afraid of using these measures and techniques. However, we do need to ensure they are used as tools and don't become an end in themselves. We also need to decide how they are used and in what context. Rightly we should regard business practices as tools to serve our mission, not as an end in themselves.

Good management practice

In seems that a distrust of professionalism and business can lead to an undervaluing of *good managerial practices* in Christian bodies.

These practices can therefore be absent or at best poorly and half-heartedly applied. This situation often seems to be made worse as we see management (as opposed to leadership) as being boring and unglamorous. As we have seen, Christian leaders can also have low awareness of management techniques and how to apply them. All of this means that the application of good management and practices is often lacking in Christian bodies. As a *consequence* of this there are a lot of people issues that go unresolved or are poorly resolved. Indeed, good managerial practices provide the foundations on which great organisations can be built.

Let's take one example. If you have good hiring practices you are likely to understand who you want to hire in terms of character, capability and ability to get on with others. You are also likely to have a good chance of getting the right person as you will understand what you're looking for and how to screen for these qualities. If you have good managerial techniques you are also likely to have role clarity and a good understanding of how a person fits with an organisation. You will also understand what they are expected to do. This not only means that you can hire the right people, but also means that the person being hired has a better chance of deciding if the role is right for them or not.

Jim Collins, in his seminal work *Good to Great*, says that one factor leading to great organisations is getting the right people on the bus and then getting them in the right seats on the bus. By this he means hiring the right people and ensuring they are in the right roles.

In Christian organisations we often see poor hiring and little understanding about role clarity. This in turn means that there is little chance of getting the right people in the right seats on the bus. Indeed, the hiring process in Christian organisations can sometimes look like all common sense has been taken out of the equation.

We see cases where people are appointed to roles regardless of if they are a fit or not, or have the skills to do the job. We see cases where the recruitment process is massively rule bound, the candidate can only be asked *x, y,* and *z* and cannot be asked *a, b, or* c (even if this information looks critical). We also see instances where only a small, fixed amount of time can used for the interview. Cases where there can only be one round of interviews, and many parties have to be involved and all these parties have different agendas. Candidates may talk of calling and this will be enough for some of the interview panel. They will accept this is the right person regardless of evidence.

So in the end, one of the most critical decisions an organisation can make is not based on good process. This will almost always *come home to roost*. The consequences of this are not only that the organisation operates in a sub-optimal way, it can also mean that real problems arise from having the wrong people in the wrong roles. Problems that, because we don't like confronting difficult issues, can detrimentally affect the organisation over a period of years.

Let's take an example. David has been recruited as senior pastor by a church. The recruitment process was not thorough and over time it becomes clear that he is not capable of leading the church. David does not know how to lead, and does not really want to lead. People want to honour and respect him, but find this harder and harder to do because of his lack of capability.

They then start to organise things around him, with others picking up much of his role and David being limited to the few things he can and will do. This kind of works but is sub-optimal, and creates a real load for others. It is also turns out to be a recipe for muddling through and not for growing the organisation as many want. Given this situation, the general level of frustration in the congregation 'rises through the roof'.

This frustration is added to by the fact that the church knows that they have the tough choice of either tackling this issue (which will be painful) or having to live with it, and all it entails, for a long time to come. As no one really knows how to grasp the issue, it is ducked. Pretty soon this lack of action has unintended consequences as Andrew, David's deputy, decides he can stand it no longer and leaves to take up another post.

The loss of Andrew means the church now has an ineffective leader, and has lost the deputy who at least kept things running. The elders now feel they have no choice but to have a 'show down' with David. At this, all the frustration which has been building up, comes pouring out. David is wounded and the elders later feel regretful. David will move on but the pain and anguish over how his exit was handled will linger. It will be a long time before the church leaves this issue behind it.

This is a story drawn from the many similar stories which we all hear—much pain is caused in the end by not being professional and demanding enough at the recruitment stage. Managerial techniques may seem mundane but properly applied they can save us from real human error in the future.

A price to pay

The introduction and maintenance of good managerial practice can involve paying a price.

This price is that these practices will demand some degree of confrontation as people are asked to adopt new habits and conform to what they may see as a demand for greater rigour. It will also have a price in that it takes hard work to introduce new systems and process and to ensure that they work properly.

Sometimes in Christian bodies we have not been prepared to pay this price. We don't like the demands it places on us and we're not always able to visualise the benefits. This is a real challenge, as a lack of preparedness to apply and abide by good systems, and a lack of rigour in what we do can mean that we don't manage the people side of our organisations as well as we could. This in turn means that we don't execute our vision as effectively as we are able.

What does all this mean for me?
Analytical tool:

It seems strange that we can often be resistant to professionalism even when embracing this might well make our organisations more effective. This seems to raise the questions 'what is it that is making us resistant'. I think part of the answer to this might well lie in the fact that embracing amateurism meets some of our own needs.

To better understand this let's look at Maslow's Hierarchy of Needs. Abraham Maslow postulated that each of us is motivated by needs. Our most basic needs are inborn, and Maslow's Hierarchy states that we must satisfy each need in turn, starting with the first, which deals with the most obvious needs for survival itself.

Only when the lower order needs of physical and emotional well-being are satisfied are we concerned with the higher order needs of influence and personal development.

Conversely, if the things that satisfy our lower order needs are swept away, we are no longer concerned about the maintenance of our higher order needs.

Maslow's model has been adapted and modified over the years but the original version remains for most people the definitive Hierarchy of Needs.

Simply stated the model is:

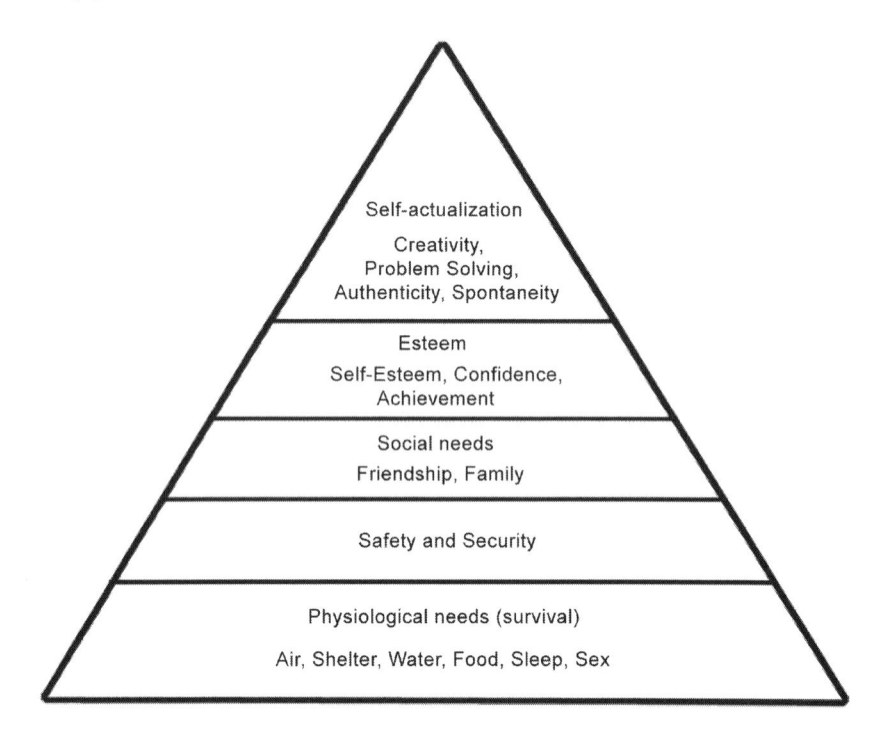

```
                    /\
                   /  \
                  /Self-\
                 /actualization\
                /  Creativity,  \
               /  Problem Solving,\
              / Authenticity, Spontaneity \
             /----------------------------\
            /           Esteem             \
           /     Self-Esteem, Confidence,   \
          /            Achievement           \
         /------------------------------------\
        /            Social needs              \
       /           Friendship, Family           \
      /------------------------------------------\
     /            Safety and Security             \
    /------------------------------------------------\
   /          Physiological needs (survival)          \
  /         Air, Shelter, Water, Food, Sleep, Sex      \
 /--------------------------------------------------------\
```

In valuing amateurism we almost seem to be stuck at level 3 of the hierarchical needs model. Amateurism in the Christian organisational context seems to mean a lack of stretch and challenge, combined with a sense of belonging and being loved, i.e. it feels safe. It's almost as if we feel that should we seek to go beyond this point and have our organisation become more professionally challenging then we fear this won't lead us to move up into having our esteem and self-actualization needs met, but will rather show us up to be somehow wanting and will mean that the love and belonging we already have is at risk!

You might think this is a large claim to make, and I agree it's a little audacious. But something keeps us wanting to remain in a comfort zone where things are a little amateur, not too demanding, and not too challenging. Professionalism and excellence have a price. They demand effort, a willingness to continually challenge and improve a situation, and an acceptance that we need to measure how we are doing. This may mean that the pursuit of professionalism and excellence can be very rewarding but will not always be comfortable and will require us to strive and to accept challenge.

Biblically, this would seem to be worthwhile both because we should give our best to God, and also because God wants us to fulfil our potential and not just do what makes us comfortable.

Story:

At a church council meeting the members reviewed the recent church carol service. This had been a rather 'rickety' and unprofessional affair. The music leader was disorganised and the choir had received their music late and once they got it they were given different versions of the same carols! There had not been the tight logistical management of previous years. Where in the past there had been readings progressing through the bible from the Old Testament to the New foretelling the birth of Christ and then the fulfilment of this promise, the format this year had seemed much less clear and perhaps less wonderful.

Despite this, the council overwhelmingly felt that it had been 'all right on the night'. People had managed to muddle through and had covered up a lot of the unprepared-ness. The congregation seem relaxed and had enjoyed a good night. When challenged about the lack of professionalism, and the fact that the congregation felt relaxed because they were mainly regular attendees and not outsiders (who might have liked more structure) coming for the first time, the majority of the council was genuinely outraged. They liked the informality and the slightly haphazard nature of the event. They did not see that in worshipping God we should give of our best in terms of organisation, preparation, and in seeking a format that would unlock the beauty of Christ's coming to this world.

The thinking of those who promoted the view that it had been a great evening was based on the fact that not being perfect is a good thing, that it relaxed people and that this kind of amateurism was attractive. This mindset was strongly held and not open to thinking that whilst we are clearly not perfect we owe our best efforts to God and His worship. It didn't take account of the fact that if a staff member takes on the organisation and leading of the music then this should be done right; to honour God, for the benefit of the congregation and to respect the time and dedication of the volunteers in the choir.

After the council meeting the unhappiness of the choir began to emerge. Unhappiness that they had been put in an invidious position by being ill prepared. In addition, the music leader's unpreparedness had an impact on other areas he had oversight of—causing poor attendance and disconnect with his volunteer team. Gradually a realisation set in that what had happened was not acceptable and the following year was a better prepared and better constructed service. This was attended by more people (including more newcomers) and from the comments afterwards, it was a service which better communicated the message of God's salvation plan to those who did not come to church on a regular basis.

So the message is we might think it's very cosy and reassuring to be slightly disorganised and amateurish, but there are immediate and long-term consequences if we allow ourselves to go too far down this route. Here I don't wish to confuse formality with professionalism. Clearly a church may have an informal approach and this will be a key part of its identity. This may well be a key strength but even informal organisation need to be supported by good professional practice. There's an interesting observation in many areas of work that where things are easy and informal for the customers, for example in a restaurant, then in order to deliver this, the people in the kitchen are really professional and organised! Similarly if we have a desire to serve our wider communities we may need to be very well organised.

CHAPTER 7

Growth

GROWTH IS NORMALLY a good thing in Christian and other organisations, and is something we welcome. Growth normally comes as a result of success; an appealing vision and strong message attract people in increasing numbers. This makes the organisation grow, and in turn it means that the organisation needs more *capacity* and *capability* to cope with success. This might mean that new and bigger premises are needed. Professional staff may need to be hired, either for the first time or in greater numbers. There may also now be larger amounts of resource and complexity to manage.

So, growth is generally to be welcomed, but in common with other charities, Christian organisations can experience difficulties around their people when they grow.

Growth tends to change the nature of the organisation. What once might have been an amateur body, which was largely run by a few enthusiastic volunteers, starts to have more paid professional people. These people start be become involved in running the organisation and the dynamics start to change.

The growth challenge looks to be greatest when an organisation goes from being small to medium sized. At this point professionalism is often introduced, and what was run on a largely informal basis becomes much more formal. Growth beyond this point, from being medium sized to large, looks less painful because by this stage the idea of professionalism has already been accepted. Moreover, this growth tends to build on existing professional processes and people.

At the stage when an organisation moves from being a small and largely voluntary organisation to needing additional professional resources a number of challenges can arise. These challenges can be at a number of levels; *individual*, *organisational*, and *governance*.

Let's take a look at what the effects of growth might be at each level.

Individual

Individuals who have been volunteers, lovingly giving time to their organisation, which they may well have helped to found, may treat with suspicion those who come to the organisation for a paid post. They may feel that they have been motivated by a calling, and here are people who seem to want to work for the organisation because it's a job. They may well intellectually see the need for hiring such people, but emotionally feel that their motivation is wrong.

Indeed there may well be a conflict of motivations between those who feel they do what they do for the organisation for *cause* as opposed to *cash*. From this a moral hierarchy of motivations may develop, and this can lead, in turn, to the dangerous implication that there is a moral hierarchy of people within the organisation. In this hierarchy, the volunteers are higher up as they are more 'pure' and the paid professionals lower down as they as merely doing a job. The introduction of paid staff can also lead to a conflict in terms of perceived competence and professionalism.

You now may have two groups; the original amateur volunteers and the new professionals. One group may regard the other as being too business-orientated and the other may regard the volunteers as lacking in skills and being unwilling to recognise their professionalism. If the professional *status* and *expertise* of the paid staff is not acknowledged and accepted by the volunteers then a potential toxic situation can emerge. In this situation the professionals may feel undervalued and sometimes undermined. On the other hand the volunteers may see these new professionals as a waste of resources, their thinking may be 'we were managing fine before we added all these expensive people!'

This dynamic all tends to be a little easier in the secular world. In business, people are paid from the outset. It is expected that part of their motivation is monetary reward, and indeed that the promised increase of these rewards will motivate people to help grow the business. The idea of being effective and efficient is also likely to be part of a business organisation's DNA, so changes to enhance this effectiveness and efficiency are easily embraced. There does not seem to be a comparable motivational conflict in a business organisation.

In charities and churches there is a much starker change when growth comes, and as we have seen, these changes can strike at core individual perceptions and values.

Organisational

In organisational terms, the introduction of paid staff can also cause conflict. This conflict can arise because people feel that prior to the employment of paid staff the resources of the church or charity were *all* directed to those who the organisation seeks to serve. However once paid staff are introduced then some of the resources of the organisation must be taken up by them. This can be an emotive issue, and can be interpreted as being wasteful by the volunteer founders of the organisation.

Professionalisation increases overheads, and therefore increases the proportion of funds that go to administration as opposed to the core work of the organisation. In the charity sector, spending money on administration can also affect donors' willingness to give. They want to see their money devoted to the key cause of the charity and not to administrative support.

The organisation, and the people who are part of it, are therefore faced with a clear issue that they must resolve. Within the organisation there needs to be unity around the idea that there is a need to build up capability and capacity to better serve its cause. People need to agree that whilst there is a moral responsibility not to waste resources, there is also a need to build systems, process and expertise that allow for growth and, in the end, increased effectiveness. This is easy to write on a piece of paper but is difficult to achieve, and these kinds of debate have debilitated more than one charitable body. Emotions can run high on both sides of the argument.

In short, the organisation really needs to understand what it is doing in this regard and have a very well thought-out and clear approach. Failing this, it will have external challenges with donors and internal challenges with people either believing money should go on developing a professional approach and systems or believing it should not. Each side is likely to be vocal and willing to 'slog it out' with the other.

Governance

Growth in Christian organisations can also cause people conflict in that as an organisation grows, governance and control has to be exercised differently.

When an organisation is small and volunteer led, governance may be very basic. This fits the needs of the organisation and allows for key decisions to be made by a small group of founders. However, as the organisation grows, employs people, develops investment plans and substantial resources, then a more formal governance process is needed. At this stage a board of trustees, or similar, is likely to be needed to ensure good stewardship.

This board may have a different perspective on life to the original founding group. They may see the need to impose new and different requirements on the organisation. They may see that now the organisation is of a certain size it needs more reporting, more formal authorisation processes, and clearer lines of responsibility than in the past. This may well conflict with the outlook of the founders and the people running the day-to-day activities. This latter group may well have enjoyed a large degree of latitude and freedom in the past, and been able to make their own decisions quickly and with little or no consultation.

The imposition of additional structures and governance may well lead to a conflict about who is really running the organisation and who is controlling its direction. A tension can develop between the trustees and the management as to who's in charge, and who is setting the direction and ensuring objectives are fulfilled.

Consider the example of an organisation that grows and has to build in greater governance. The new board of trustees want more reporting, measuring, accountability, more planning and more approvals to be sought up-front. The team running the organisation want to get on and run it as they always have. They feel that they should be allowed to run the operation with the minimum supervision, and indeed the board should really play the role of enthusiastic supporter.

In this situation the stage is set for conflict, strained relationships, and for each party to misinterpret the motives of the other. In this atmosphere a lack of trusts develops and the slightest error on either side could lead to suspicion, crisis and bad blood. In view of this, organisationally, growth needs to be handled in a careful manner. There needs to be real consultation and from this a unity of purpose and direction needs to emerge. Even then this will not be enough. All parties will need to be committed to making the new structures and processes work, and will need to renew this commitment every day until the changes are 'bedded in.'

The culture of an organisation may also change as growth takes place. This growth, and the professionalisation it brings, will lead to a challenge to the basic assumptions of the organisation. It will raise questions of who is the organisation for, who is it accountable to, and who is leading it? The organisation, and the people within it, need to be prepared for these questions, and also be prepared to address them together. If not they can cause a lot of pain and anguish.

What does all this mean for me?
Analytical tool:

All organisations experience a life cycle and growth is a part of this. Adizes identified ten stages of corporate life. His single-word descriptions are quite self-explanatory for many people's understanding, which is part of the model's appeal and elegance. Below this first list I've extended the model with some brief interpretation and descriptive examples of each stage.

1. courtship
2. infancy
3. go-go
4. adolescence
5. prime
6. stability
7. aristocracy
8. recrimination
9. bureaucracy
10. death

Terms explanations and examples:

1. courtship (the initial development or creation of the proposition/model/business/formation/etc)
2. infancy (after launch—start of active trading)
3. go-go (frantic, energetic early growth and sometimes chaos)
4. adolescence (still developing but more established and defined)
5. prime (the business or organisation at its fittest, healthiest and most competitive, popular and profitable)
6. stability (still effective, popular, can still be very profitable, but beginning to lose leading edge—vulnerability may be creeping in)
7. aristocracy (strong by virtue of market presence and consolidated accumulated successes, but slow and unexciting, definitely losing market share to competitors and new technologies, trends, etc)

8. recrimination (doubts, problems, threats and internal issues overshadow the original purposes)

9. bureaucracy (inward-focused administration, cumbersome, seeking exit or divestment, many operating and marketing challenges)

10. death (closure, sell-off, bankruptcy, bought for asset value or customer-base only)

I offer this model as an awareness tool—it helps show and number of things:

- Life cycles are normal, things cannot stay static and change needs to be accepted
- It's critical to be aware of where your organisation is on the cycle—this allows you to manage your circumstances
- Most importantly it's important to know when you've reached the top of the cycle (stages 5/6)—this means you can be aware of when you need to fundamentally re-generate the organisation

Story:

This story concerns a charity formed in Africa with UK support to alleviate child poverty and neglect. The charity is formed by a British man and his wife. Between them the couple are experienced in social work and education. They start out with a clear understanding of the need for professionalism in the work they deliver in terms of social counselling for the children, the provision of education and the provision of medical support. This ethos of providing professional support is underlined as appropriately trained staff are recruited from the west. Local staff are also recruited and developed to ensure the children are well supported as they are given a home, help and education to move on from being abandoned and abused.

For the first four years the charity grows from a very small beginning and becomes recognised for the positive work it's carrying out. The team on the ground forms a close knit family who have a high sense of calling for their work and a commonly shared view not only about the importance of what they are doing but also how it should be done. In short they feel that the work on the ground is what matters and they are much less interested in the 'bureaucratic' needs of the organisation such as book-keeping and administration. They are highly focused on their children and their mission and as a team they enjoy strong relationships. These are seen as the things that matter and also the route to resolve any problems which the organisation faces.

In time, as the organisation grows, its leader comes under enormous work pressure. This person is taking part in and guiding the work, leading the team and managing all the aspects of the charity's life with the exception of the UK based fund-raising operation. The load is just too much and even this person, who is not keen to let go of responsibility (in case this somehow kills the essence of the charity) realises that he must get some help. There is also a realisation that the help needed is managerial and administrative, and that this area must be properly addressed. In time it appears this realisation was more of a head than a heart realisation.

After an extensive search a seemingly ideal person, who is known to many of the key players, is hired. This person starts work but soon begins to feel discouraged. He finds he is like a newcomer to a family where everyone else is very clear of their role and place but where his role has not been made clear to anyone. The staff team continues to go to the leader with all their issues, even the ones concerning the administration of the charity, and the leader (rather than referring them to the new man) keeps on dealing with these issues. Pretty soon the new guy is being by-passed.

In addition, it's also not clear what the new manager's decision-making authority is, if any. Finally, the new manager fails as he tries to introduce new systems and processes to help the charity move forward and to accommodate its need for greater reporting and controls as it grows. He is frustrated in this work as the existing family do not see the need for these things, being happy with the way things are, and therefore don't want to invest their time in helping to build these processes. The manager feels he cannot make this situation work and that he has no option but to leave. This process all took place over a two-year period, and was rooted in a lack of agreement about how growth should be handled and resourced.

The same charity next faced a subsequent issue, the issue being that 'old chestnut' question—'who's in charge?' As the organisation grew, so the UK board of trustees and UK based staff wanted a greater say in how it was run and governed. They no longer wanted to be a support group for the fieldwork in Africa, they wanted to take a greater part in strategy and direction. This desire for greater involvement took on a number of forms.

Firstly a job was created in the UK which had parity with the field head (the effective founder of the charity). This role focused on the UK side of the work, fund raising and building the charity's image. The first appointment to this role was made by the UK team, with no involvement from the field head. Things did not go well, the trustees came to realise that the appointee was the wrong person for the role, and the founder saw no need for the role, felt disenfranchised by the process and could not believe who had been appointed. This mess took over a year to resolve until the trustees worked out that they had no option but to exit this person—with a generous package.

Still feeling the need to appoint a person in the UK, the trustees now decided to try again to fill the role. This time the field head was involved, more care was taken and a recognised professional was appointed. This person had real skills, experience and expertise and as a consequence of this she not only had a view as to how to develop the UK support side of things, she also had a view about how things should be conducted on the ground in Africa. Not surprisingly, pretty soon she and the field head were rubbing each other up the wrong way. She actually had more development experience and was a recognised development professional, he had the experience on the ground, had build the charity up and had a high degree of ownership for what was happening. She wanted to use her expert knowledge for the benefit of the organisation and also wanted to be valued for expertise. When she found that she had no real access to the core work of the charity she left.

Finally, the who's in charge debate centred on the role of the trustees. This body had originally consisted of friends and supporters of the founder and had acted as a money raising team who saw themselves as cheerleaders for the work. As the organisation grew and new trustees came on board, who were not connected with the founder, they wanted to fulfil a real governance role. This inevitably meant a conflict between the trustees and founder and his field team, who partly wanted to retain control and partly were frustrated by what they saw as additional bureaucracy. This tension was worked on and ameliorated but never really resolved until the cast of characters—field head, board chair, other trustees changed over time and a new generation, who did not have the history and emotional investment of the earlier generation, took over.

Change is tough to handle but as organisations grow and professionalise there is a need to agree what value new professionals will add to the body, what their role is, and there also needs to be agreement that they will be allowed to contribute. In terms of authority and governance this also needs to be clear—those who are executing the work of the organisation on the ground need to be accountable but also need to be left with enough of the day-to-day decision making to be effective.

CHAPTER 8

Volunteerism

O NE KEY DIFFERENCE in the Christian and not for profit world, compared to the business world, is that there is often a high reliance on volunteers. Volunteers tend to be critical to the organisation and the dynamics of leading and working with this population can be very different from working with a paid staff.

One of my interviewees summed this up very neatly by saying it's like the difference between a South American bolas and a set of planets circling a sun. A bolas is a series of balls that are attached to the central point by rope, whereas the planets only circle the sun because of gravitational force.

The bolas is like an organisation with a paid staff. These people are related and linked to the centre by strong ties, normally in the form of contracts, job security and payment. Volunteers are more like the planets. They are held in place by a less tangible force and may spin off if this gravitational pull weakens. With volunteers, this gravity or attraction to the centre is normally as a result of attraction to the vision, values and leadership of the organisation. This can be reinforced if they also find significance and purpose in what they are doing. However, it can also mean that the attraction to the centre can be reduced if the volunteer perceives that things are not being done as they would like or in a way which motivates them.

Expectations

Leading and managing volunteers can be complex and challenging for many reasons. At its most basic, volunteers do not need to serve in an organisation, they choose to do so. This dynamic makes some leaders feel that they cannot expect too much of the volunteer. They cannot ask them to deliver too much, be on time or meet the standards that they would normally expect from paid staff.

They feel that they should be grateful for anything the volunteer gives them, even if a lack of reliability hurts the organisation and its performance. In addition to this, leaders can also develop a mind-set that says 'we don't want to upset Harry or Amanda, if we do they will take their bat home.' They think 'we'll never see them again and it's better to have them here delivering even a little than to lose them for good.'

In most Christian organisations there is often more work to do than there are people available to do it. This shortage of talent and need to get the roles filled can lead us to appoint unqualified volunteers. Often we do this even into key roles that demand a high degree of expertise. Indeed, it sometimes feels like the person you really want in a role is not available because due to their talent they are already very busy running the United Nations, the IMF or the like. As a result of this we then turn to someone who is available but may well not be the right person.

A good example of this tendency is the appointments to the treasure role. The organisation has an income of half a million dollars and employs staff. The treasurer role is voluntary but due to it onerous nature and heavy responsibilities it's been hard to find anyone. Eventually, Jim steps forward to take up the role. He doesn't really want to do it and feels unqualified but he is trying to be a good soldier and fill a gap that no one else will take up. He does not have a financial background, and has little understanding of the duties and obligations of an employer. He's a writer working out of his home. He's persuaded that this role can fit around his writing and that he can make it work because 'he should have the time to do it.'

He struggles through but over time the organisation suffers as time and energy keeps being sucked in to fighting financial and administrative fires and not focusing on core purpose and vision. Because he can't get on top of the bookkeeping, issues keep popping up which were unexpected and it's very hard to get accurate data on which to make any judgements. Jim feels beleaguered and his colleagues start to feel frustrated that they always seem to be clearing up problems, or revisiting financial issues which they thought were closed. No one is happy and the tensions begin to show.

This mismatch is not limited to the treasurer's role. It can also be seen in governance roles where volunteers are appointed to oversee an organisation but do not understand governance, finance, human resources, planning or any of the skills they require to effectively undertake the job. This can lead to stresses and strains, especially if they are serving with people who understand these things and want to move the organisation forward. This latter group feels held back by those who do not have the experience to understand the challenges in front of them and what the organisation needs to do next. In this situation personal relationships are likely to suffer and the atmosphere can become difficult.

Motivation

Another key challenge is that volunteers are sometimes motivated by their own needs and agendas and therefore may not fully align and commit to those of the organisation.

Volunteers often join organisations for non-financial rewards. Instead they are looking to be recognised, and to do what they feel is important. They may also seek a form of self-actualisation and significance.

Let's take the example of Lucy. She wants to undertake God's work and volunteers to serve in a Christian organisation. She has a particular view of what it means to undertake God's work and does not see a need to test this against the views, or needs, of the organisation. Her real need is to fulfil her own agenda, if this fits with the needs of the organisation then well and good, if not then she's going to go in her direction regardless.

Lucy feels that because she is not paid, that the organisation should be willing to fit in with what she is willing to give. In her heart of hearts she really does not want to be held accountable by the organisation. She feels that the deal really is that in exchange for volunteering, she will be given lots of freedom to do what she thinks is right. She not only expects very little challenge, she expects lots of encouragement and support. She is convinced that she is working for the best, and moreover is giving her time freely. In view of this what she gives should be accepted gratefully and without challenge.

Lucy's case is not uncommon and shows us that there can be a real complexity and lack of clarity with regards to the deal between volunteers and the organisation. This can lead to *great* frustration on both sides. One person I interviewed described managing volunteers as a 'nightmare'. The organisation is frustrated by their lack of reliability, delivery and alignment and the volunteers are frustrated as they feel that they are not being allowed to do their own thing and are not getting the recognition they deserve.

Consultation and communication

Volunteers often expect a high degree of consultation. Pretty much everyone expects to be consulted on everything whether it has anything to do with them or not. This can be regardless of whether or not they can add anything to the issue. This *being involved* seems to be part of the *compensation* which volunteers look for. It is part of people feeling significant, involved and attached to the organisation.

Consultation may be expected, but it does add an additional challenge for Christian and voluntary leaders. The key element of that challenge is *time*. It seems to be true that if you're a leader of such an organisation you should expect things to take a long time. You often have to get everyone signed up and on board before you can get a new project to take off. Not only this, but you can also be sure that everyone will have a view and opinion which will need to be worked through. Think again of the picture of the planets around the sun. They are held in place by gravity and in a voluntary organisation you have to keep working to ensure this gravity stays intact, and the planets do not fly off into space.

This need to consult does not mean people are obstructive. Rather it means they want to be acknowledged and heard. There looks to be evidence that volunteers value being consulted and if this happens they are willing to adopt a new course of action. Often they will be willing to embrace this even if it is not the one they lobbied for. It seems that sometimes being consulted is more important than the outcome. It's about significance and being valued. It is not unheard of in Christian organisations that we get ourselves into trouble (and strife) by not investing enough time in the consultation process.

I was once part of a process where we had the most heated and protracted exchange regarding how we should change the church logo. All seemed to agree that the logo should be changed and one group felt that this was a fairly simple process. They thought that we would give a member of the congregation (who had the appropriate set of skills) the task of having some new designs generated and that we would then chose from these and get on with the change. This group was in 'the driving seat' on the issue so this methodology was adopted. The different options were worked up and brought a council meeting and then opposition started to emerge. There was a group that didn't like any of the proposed new designs, they wanted to get their own designs, they wanted the issue to have far more consideration. Huge frustrations and even anger started to emerge on both sides; one side thinking the other had lost all sense of reasoning and was making a 'mountain out of a molehill' and the other wanting to see more debate and input. Unbelievably this issue dragged on for many council meetings, generating heat at each one until eventually everyone became embarrassed at the amount of time, energy and emotion this had consumed; the go ahead was eventually given to the design which had been first floated. This embarrassment was added to as the congregation had got wind of this debate and were standing by open mouthed at what they saw as a crazy and colossal waste of time being given to a minor issue.

Looking back at that incident I tried to unpack what had happened and where all the emotion had come from. My conclusion was that the issue was not the *design* of the logo but the *consultation* process. One group started to feel, at a fundamental level, that they were being 'railroaded' by the group who wanted a quick change. They did not feel consulted and thought that there was some kind of power play afoot. As a consequence this minor issue evolved into 'logo wars' as one wag described it. Everyone could see how foolish this was but it showed that if you want volunteers on board, then time spent on consultation and obtaining buy in is time well spent.

With regard to communication, it is just worth remembering that when you're outlining a new idea to a group, then different people will need to hear the idea in different ways and through different media. Indeed, don't be surprised if people don't get the idea until you have repeated it many times. I know leaders are surprised when they have cast a new idea for the tenth time and people come up to them as if they have just heard it or say 'thanks for doing that, I now get it; I heard it before but I didn't get it.'

In terms of different styles and media, don't be afraid to use stories, symbols, slogans, drawings or humour to communicate messages. We once made one of our most successful and effective financial appeals by producing a mock (pink!) copy of the Financial Times for the congregation containing stories and humour. Everyone remembers this appeal—so be prepared to use a variety of media and innovative ideas to reach your people.

The need for many people to agree

In a business environment, many people may be consulted on a course of action but ultimately few need to agree it. The CEO alone, or with some other senior colleagues, will usually set the direction or make a decision about how to handle an issue which has arisen and has been investigated.

In the Christian and voluntary world it is often true that governance and good practice mean that many people must *agree* before a course of action can be embarked upon. These people may be staff, trustees or volunteers, but whatever they are, it's likely that their input has to be sought and some level of agreement reached. This not only adds a time challenge and means that the organisation may not be 'fleet of foot', it also means that many compromises and changes may have to be built into a piece of work so that it has enough support and consensus to be undertaken. This may enhance the piece of work, but more likely it will detract from the quality of what's done. There is a classic saying that a camel is a horse designed by a committee. Christian organisations can suffer from the idea that everyone has to have a say in how something is done, and because if this, the issue in question is often handled less clearly and effectively than it could have been.

A double-sided coin

In this chapter I have talked a lot about the challenges of managing a voluntary organisation. I don't want to close without also saying what many interviewees said to me. That is, whilst there are many challenges there is also huge strength to be found in the voluntary sector. Often we find very committed and skilled individuals delivering exceptional levels of performance. This is why volunteers are a double-sided coin, they can be challenging but they can also be terrific. The question is how do you unlock the fantastic contribution volunteers can make? This contribution can benefit the organisation and provide high levels of satisfaction to the individuals involved. As in so many things, the answer appears to lie in being clear from the outset; clear about your expectations of the volunteers, clear as to the qualities and skills you need, and a willingness to keep looking until you get the right fit. If we remember that old adage in recruiting, 'if in doubt don't hire', that we mentioned before, the same looks true with volunteers.

What does all this mean for me? Analytical tool:

Here's an analytical tool based on the work of Marcus Buckingham and Kurt Coffman in their book *First Break All the Rules*. It's a way of gauging **engagement** and could be used with volunteers (and also staff) to see if you have got buy-in and have won their hearts and minds in terms of commitment to and alignment with the organisation and its goals.

Core Elements To Attract, Focus And Keep Talented Good People

1. Do I know what the organisation expects of me?
2. Do I have the equipment and materials needed to do my work right?
3. Do I have the opportunity to do what I do best every day?
4. In the last seven days have I received praise or recognition for good work?
5. Does the person I report to seem to care about seem to care about me as a person?
6. Is there someone in the organisation who encourages my development?
7. Do my opinions seem to count in the organisation?
8. Does the mission/purpose of my organisation make me feel like my work is important?
9. Are my co-workers committed to doing quality work?
10. Do I have a best friend in the organisation?
11. In the last six months have I talked about my progress with someone in the organisation?
12. This last year have I had opportunities to learn and grow?

Story:

This story concerns communicating effectively to volunteers, and properly empowering them. Jill was selected to head up the church's evangelism work. She had retired early and had time available and moreover she appeared to have a vision for this area. This vision was to bring a greater evangelism element to the church's many outreach events. These had generally become socials to which people were invited to build relationships and to show that Christians were normal people who didn't have two heads. The process worked reasonably well, in that non-Christians liked to come to the events including balls, quizzes, curry nights and golf days. They also liked to know that the money they paid to attend and the funds raised went to charities, such as schools in Africa, local advice centres for pregnant women, micro-finance charities and the like.

What was missing was that attendance at these events did not often convert into people coming to church. In fact in some cases people weren't really clear about who had sponsored and organised the event!

Jill was willing to tackle this by making sure all events contained an evangelistic piece and also by ensuring that the church and its services were profiled. She realised this needed to be done in an appropriate way and had to avoid being 'heavy-handed'. Many in the church family realised this area needed addressing and were happy that the pastor approached Jill and asked her to lead this area and create a small team to support the work.

Months passed and nothing appeared to be happening. People began to ask how it was all going. Jill's reply to these enquiries was that it was correct that the pastor had asked her to lead this work, and that she was enthusiastic to do so. However following a brief initial discussion the pastor had not followed up with her to outline in more detail what he wanted, how he saw this working and the milestones he hoped would be met. The pastor had assumed after their initial chat that Jill would just 'get on with it' and make the whole process work. There are some volunteers who, once they have been given the most limited briefing, will make it all happen, but they a few in number. To be truly empowered most people need some clear guidelines and regular reviews. If they don't get this they can be paralysed and do nothing as they feel that they've been asked to roller skate in the dark on top of skyscraper. They don't want to move because there is such a lack of clarity. Jill, who incidentally had a strong scientific and fact-based background, felt this way. She was willing to act but wanted guidelines and reporting to be in place in order to move forward. As both of these were lacking, despite requests for them, she did not move and the whole initiative stalled.

The point here for leaders is that good volunteers may want real empowerment before they move. They want to know how you want things done, to have regular contact with you as the process develops, and to know (through regular inputs) that they have your support. They probably don't want to be micro-managed, part of their motivation will be to have some ownership of the area, but they do want guidelines, targets and monthly communication. Getting the best from volunteers can mean the leader has to invest wisely in them and the work they have been asked to do.

PART TWO

CHAPTER 9

What Did Jesus Do?

In the first part of this book we took a look at why we struggle with the people issues. There seems to be a number of reasons for this, from relational complexity, to personal agendas, to our human shortcomings and the challenges that growth and volunteerism provide.

Often this struggle seems to be because we shy away from providing clarity with regard to expectations and because we're uncomfortable confronting difficult issues. Sometimes, we seem to find it hard to be honest with one another and value pretty superficial relationships, and the pretence that everything is OK, more than being open with each other. We can find it hard to have enough trust to enter into real and grown up relationships with each other. There are also times when we seem to value our own agendas and needs more highly than those of the other people in our organisations.

Our motivation for all this is not usually sinister. In fact it seems to spring from a desire to be nice, to treat each other compassionately, or from a genuine blindness as to our own behaviour. We often seem to get ourselves in that classic dilemma of doing all the wrong things for what we think are the right reasons!

Given this, we probably need a better model for our interactions and relationships than a belief in human niceness. As we have a shared faith based on the idea that Christ offered himself as a sacrifice to save us from our sins, it seems sensible that we should look to his example of human interaction and leadership.

Mission

Jesus came from heaven to earth with a clear mission, a mission beautifully described in John 3:16, 'for God so loved the world that he gave his one and only Son, that whoever believes in him shall not perish but have eternal life.' Jesus comes to earth to fulfil God's rescue plan for mankind.

At the fall, humanity sinned; we were not capable of maintaining the paradise provided for us, and were incapable of throwing off our sinful nature. Because God is a just God there is a price to pay for this, a price we should individually bear. However, God is merciful as well as just and so He sent his only Son to pay the price for our sins! A situation often likened to being in court and finding someone else is prepared to take on our sentence.

Jesus had a clear mission to save mankind by dying in our place. We are called to respond by believing in him, and being faithful. If we do this we will be granted eternal life. We also know that the other part of Jesus' mission is to come again at the end of this world when he will judge the living and the dead. We will be judged according to faith; have we accepted him as our personal saviour? We cannot save ourselves by good works, but only by faith. Faith of course is likely to lead to good works, but firstly we must have the belief.

Jesus' mission sets us, as Christians, our own mission. We are challenged to mirror his purpose and example in our own lives. Our mission looks to be firstly to repent and express gratitude, in the form of praise for what God has done for us in saving us from our own sins. Secondly, part of this gratitude should be to accept Jesus into our lives and to seek to follow his example. Our lives should be transformed and we should live out his truths. Like the woman in John 8:11, we are told to 'go now and leave your life of sin.' Through this we aim to give glory to God, and live lives that are righteous and healthy in His sight, by the power of His ever-present Holy Spirit. We are called to be salt and light, a positive example to those around us. We also are called to spread the good news about Jesus to others and by doing so enable them to obtain eternal life through their own faith.

Action

Jesus not only came to earth to fulfil his solo mission. He also worked with and through people. He demonstrated who he was through the testimony of others, the miracles he performed and his teaching. He provided a perfect example to the world, an example of what must come first; love of God, and how to live out this love; by treating our fellow humans as ourselves, and how to lead; by serving. He modelled the way for us all. He was also prepared to provide healthy challenge to those around him, both supporters and detractors, not only to point to the error of their ways but also to show the right road to travel on.

By faith, we too need to respond with actions that should be a mirror of Jesus' ministry. We need to validate that we're authentic to others in the ways that we behave. Bickering and division is not a great example, whereas small and large acts of kindness are a reflection of the love of God.

We need to set an example both in the way we live our lives as individuals and the way we operate corporately. We should also be prepared to offer healthy challenge in order to help keep people off the wrong route and on the right one.

Let's now take a look in more detail at the example Jesus gives us. Let's particularly examine how this example relates to our interactions with others and how to create good and authentic relationships.

CHAPTER 10

Authority and Expectations

WHEN WE LOOK at the New Testament, Jesus' authority does not seem to be in doubt. He certainly has no doubt about his own authority and who he is. We see this authority underlined in many places and by many different voices, including by the voice of God Himself. In Luke 9, Jesus is transfigured and is joined by Moses and Elijah on the mountain. In Luke 9:34 a cloud envelops Jesus (and the disciples who are present) and in 9:35 God the Father says of Jesus, 'this is my Son, whom I have chosen; listen to him.' This echoes the scene in Mark 1:11 when Jesus emerges from the waters of the Jordan and God the Father says to him, 'you are my Son, whom I love; with you I am well pleased.' God Himself confirms who Jesus is and publically bestows authority upon him.

In John 1:29-30, John the Baptist also identifies Jesus and talks of his purpose and authority saying, 'look, the Lamb of God, who takes away the sin of the world! This is the one I meant when I said, 'A man who comes after me has surpassed me because he was before me' and in Matthew 2:2 the Magi show they know who Jesus is when they ask, 'where is the one who has been born King of the Jews?'

Jesus, therefore, has real authority and he is prepared to use this authority to set high expectations of others. In Matthew 4:19–22 we see Jesus calling the disciples. In this passage we can see that he expects that they will follow him without question. He expects them to give up everything; their jobs, their homes and their families to answer his call.

This is not a 'one off' event and later in Matthew 10:37-39 we see Jesus setting the bar high for his followers. Here he says, 'anyone who loves his father or mother more than me is not worthy of me; anyone who loves his son or daughter more than me is not worthy of me; and anyone who does not take up his cross and follow me is not worthy of me. Whoever finds his life will lose it, and whoever loses his life for my sake will find it.' He is saying that he needs to come first in the life of his disciples, above all others, and that they need to be prepared to embrace a difficult and challenging life in order to fully follow him.

We are also given a beautiful story of authority and expectation in the story of the faithful Centurion. In Luke 7:1-10 we see this story unfold. The Centurion has a sick servant whom he values highly, and he asks the Jewish elders to go to Jesus to ask him to heal this servant. The Centurion is a representative of the occupying power, Rome, but he has treated Israel well and has even built a synagogue. Jesus responds to the entreaties of the elders and agrees to go to the Centurion's house to heal the servant.

Next we see something really extraordinary, the Centurion realising how difficult it will be for Jesus to enter his house, the house of a Gentile, sends a friend to him to say, 'Lord, don't trouble yourself, for I do not deserve you under my roof. That is why I did not even consider myself worthy to come to you. But say the word, and my servant will be healed. For I myself am a man under authority, with soldiers under me. I tell this one, 'Go' and he goes; and that one, 'Come', and he comes,' Luke 7:6-8. This man fully recognises Jesus' authority, and because of this he fully expects that he will be able to heal the servant by just saying the word. Jesus is amazed at what he hears and says to the crowd who are with him, 'I tell you, I have not found such great faith even in Israel.' Jesus is commending this faith, this acknowledgement of his authority, and the expectation of the Centurion is fulfilled as his servant is made well.

What does all this tell us as we try and think through how we might manage the people side of things better? Well, it tells us that some are given real authority and that provided that this is legitimate then it should be respected. It also tells us that those who have authority should not be afraid to set clear and demanding expectations. Jesus is certainly not afraid of being very clear with those around him, he's not afraid of setting sky high expectations and setting these standards with very natural ease, and authority.

If we consider the issue of alignment, which we talked about earlier, maybe this model shows us a couple of things. Firstly, those in authority should set and expect alignment to their goals. It also shows us that we need to be careful of multiple personal agendas, and that we should seek to adjust our own needs to those of the wider organisation.

In terms of accountability, Jesus is also clear that this quality is expected and that we are required to answer for our activities. In Luke 11:52 he demonstrates this when he makes it clear that teachers of the law carry real responsibilities and but have fallen short of these. Here he says, 'woe to you experts in the law, because you have taken away the key to knowledge. You yourselves have not entered, and you have hindered those who were entering.' Basically, this is saying, 'you took on key responsibilities and have not delivered, and there will be consequences.'

Responsibility and accountability are also highlighted in Luke 12:48 where Jesus also makes it plain that if you have received a lot you will be required to give a lot back. In this passage Jesus says, 'from everyone who has been given much, much will be demanded; and from the one who has been entrusted with much, much more will be asked.' Following this, in Luke 19:12–27 we then see this idea reinforced by the story of the Ten Minas.

Ten servants are each given a mina by a rich man who leaves for another land to be crowned king. When he returns each is asked what they have done with the money, the first three appear before him. One has increased it ten fold, one has made a five fold increase and the third has 'kept it safe' and done nothing with it. The two who have used what they were given to good effect are praised and rewarded the last one is chastised and his mina is taken from him and given to the one who has made the best return. This may seem a tough story but the implications are clear, we are expected to use what we are given as well as can, in so doing we honour God, and if we fail to do this we will have to answer for our actions. In short we will be entrusted with talents and resources by God but are expected to use these wisely, and to be prepared to be accountable for what we do with them.

Given this example, it seems that we should not shy away from accountability, and should be prepared to hold others accountable. In a way these two concepts keep each other in check, because we are accountable we know we cannot abuse our right to hold others accountable and must do this in a way that would honour God.

So, the first thing we see is that Jesus is a leader with real authority, and a leader who is prepared to use this authority to set the highest standards. He is also a leader who shows that there are rewards and consequences for our actions, especially if we have been given a lot or if we are in a key role. This is a level of clarity and expectation we often fail to demonstrate in our own organisations. It's a model of leadership that many would find it difficult to meet, and yet it is the model we are offered by our saviour. More than this, Jesus is so clear and his expectations are so high because he is seeking the salvation of people, and this mission is of such high importance. He knows that there must be clarity, there must be expectations, standards and accountability, and that issues should not be ducked.

One last word on authority; Jesus is a leader who understands empowerment and the passing on of authority, and by implication understands his hierarchical powers. In Mark 3:13–15 he appoints the twelve and defines the powers they will have. Similarly, in Luke 10:1-16, he appoints the seventy-two and explains what their mission is and how they should behave, he empowers them to speak in his name.

He also recognises when he does not have authority or cannot alter a situation, in Mark 10:40 he says to James and John, 'but to sit at my right or left is not for me to grant. These places belong to those for whom they have been prepared.' In Luke 22:42 he says to God, 'Father, if you are willing take this cup from me; yet not my will but yours be done.' Here, as one in authority, he also understands he is under authority and models this.

Here we get a validation of a right hierarchy and a great leadership model, of authority, clarity, expectations and submission.

CHAPTER 11

Tough Love

In the Christian psyche we sometimes seem to struggle with the idea that *compassion* and being *tough* can exist in the same space. We often don't seem to understand that if we love someone enough we can also be very clear with them about the standards required, and what is and is not acceptable. If we really value someone, and they know this, then we can tell them when they are off-track, and moreover we're likely to do this in an appropriate and helpful way.

Scripture contains many examples of Jesus' compassion. In Mark 1:41 we're told that Jesus is, 'filled with compassion' for the leper and heals him. In Luke 8:48 we see the wonderful story of Jesus and the woman in the crowd. In this passage a woman who has been bleeding for twelve years, comes up and secretly touches his cloak, and is healed. She is suffering from a humiliating condition, she has tried everything to cure it, nothing has worked and we can assume that this has pushed her to the margins of society as her condition would be regarded as unclean and distasteful by those who came into contact with her. Jesus shows his compassion for the woman not so much in his healing of her, as we see he initially appears to be unaware of who has touched him. In fact he asked who touched him, explaining that he felt the power go out from him. His compassion is really fully demonstrated when she comes forward to admit that it was she who touched his cloak and how she had been instantly healed. Here she is admitting not only that she touched him but also making her condition public to the crowd. Jesus then says to her, 'Daughter, your faith has healed you. Go in peace.' By doing this he is not only confirms her healing but he honours her by referring to her as daughter. Here he is making it clear she is not an outcast any longer, and that in his eyes she enjoys the high status of family member. He ensures she is socially restored.

Peter is regarded with much fondness by many. He is the disciple who often shows great enthusiasm and many human failings. Because of this we find it easy to identify with him and can sympathise with him when he is bewildered by some new challenge or concept. Unfortunately, his very human qualities lead him to deny his Lord three times when Jesus is arrested. Jesus foretold that this would happen and as soon as the third denial escapes his lips, Peter knows that this is the blunder of all blunders. However, despite this, we see in John 21:15-19 the remarkable compassion of Jesus, as the risen Christ reinstates Peter as his follower three times. He gives Peter a fresh chance and a new beginning. He commissions Peter to 'Feed my lambs' to 'Take care of my sheep' and to 'Follow me.'

This theme of compassion is also demonstrated in Matthew 14:14 where we hear how Jesus had compassion on the crowd and healed the sick. Perhaps most significantly in John 15:13 he gives a foretaste of the enormous compassion he will show for humanity saying, 'greater love has no man than this, that he lays down his life for his friends.' Here he foreshadows the crucifixion saying that he will give his own life to take away the sins of the world, that he will pay the price that is owed for man's transgressions, and that he will settle humanity's debt with God. Here is the most compassionate act possible, to sacrifice oneself for others.

However, in spite of this compassion, or more accurately because of it, Jesus does exercise some real toughness and clarity with those around him. Crucially this toughness is not reserved for those who are seeking to attack him and bring him down, it is also directed at those for whom he has great compassion and love.

In Matthew 19:16-24 we can read the wonderful and challenging story of the Rich Young Man. In this story a rich young man comes to Jesus wanting to understand what he must do to get eternal life. Jesus says he should keep all the commandments. On hearing this, the young man says he has kept the commandments, and asks what else he still needs to do. Jesus then gives him a real challenge saying, 'go and sell your possessions and give to the poor, and you will have treasure in heaven. Then come, follow me.' He's effectively saying to the young man, here's your chance to go down the right road but there is a price to pay. I want the best for you but it won't be easy and will involve sacrifice. Jesus values this person enough to give him a full and clear answer, and a challenge. Here we see really tough love; there is a compassion and love for the man, but also a challenging and tough message is given to him.

We again see this compassion and toughness in the story of the Paralytic. In this famous story the man's friends bring him to Jesus to be cured. They lower him through the roof where Jesus is, as the crowd is too great for them to get in through the door. In Mark 2:5 Jesus forgives him his sins, but does not seem to cure his physical ailment. Here he is showing real compassion as he is granting the man what he really needs, rather than what he and his friends may be seeking. Later, in Mark 2:11 he also cures him physically, but he does this to demonstrate his authority to the teachers of the law. This story is an interesting example of tough love; of giving what's really needed rather than what others may think they want.

Jesus also calls out the behaviour of his disciples and is prepared to be pretty tough with them. In Mark 7:18 we see him saying to the disciples, 'are you so dull?' He challenges them to understand what he has been saying about what makes a man clean or unclean, his point being that it is what comes from within that is the problem, not, as in this case, externally consumed food. Effectively, he is here saying to the disciples, come on guys, you have to step up here and start to really understand what I have been saying.

Nicodemus is a sympathetic figure in the bible. He is a Pharisee and member of the elite, but also someone who seems to really want to understand and honour Jesus. In John 3:1-21 we see him going to Jesus (albeit under the cover of darkness) to try and understand more fully his message and who he is. Jesus talks to him of the need to be 'born again' in the Spirit. This is beyond the comprehension of Nicodemus who can't understand how a man can be born a second time. In verses 10-21 of chapter 3, Nicodemus ends up getting a tough message from Christ. The message says, 'look I have tried to explain to you, but you don't really understand what I am trying to tell you, and as a consequence you will continue to live in darkness.'

In Luke 10:41-42 we see some further clear guidance from Jesus to a friend. Martha comes to complain to him that her sister Mary is sitting around listening to him when she should be helping her get the meal ready. Jesus responds by telling her that her sister Mary has made the better choice in listening to him, rather than preparing the meal. This is probably not the intervention Martha has been expecting and it must have sent her away a little perplexed. However again we see Jesus valuing her by being clear with her about what is and is not important. He's trying to give her the best guidance possible.

In Luke 19:1-9 we get the great story of Zacchaeus the tax collector. This reviled figure wants to see Jesus. He's small and so has to climb up a tree in order to be able to see him over the heads of the crowd. When Jesus reaches his tree he calls out to him saying he must stay at Zacchaeus' house. Jesus showed him compassion by recognising him and in return for this Zacchaeus knows he has to offer a real response. This response was to give up some of what he had valued most—his money—and to change his ways and deal with people in an honest and straight way. Here again we see the elements of tough love, Jesus offers Zacchaeus a new start, but there is a price, something of value must be given up and the new start must be genuine and followed through.

In the person of Jesus, then, we can see that compassion and toughness can co-exist. In fact, more than this, it's clear that they not only co-exist but are really two halves of the same equation. Both compassion and love, plus a willingness to be clear and tough, are needed if we are to have real relationships with one another. We must also be able to speak the truth in love. If we can't do this then our relationships will be limited and potentially superficial, and they may not be of a quality whereby we can really help and support each other. Christ modelled this behaviour. He not only challenged the Pharisees and his antagonists, he was also very clear with those closest to him and those he wanted to help.

Perhaps this can be a model for us in our own interactions. It can encourage us to have real relationships, to move beyond just being nice, and by blending compassion and toughness to move to real, supportive and honest relationships. This is clearly not easy to do, but it's also not impossible. Think what your organisation would be like if you reached this state, in fact take a look at people and organisations who act this way and see the richness of their communities.

One word of caution, we have to really value other people to get to a truly effective state. We can't just try a little to like them and then think this is enough of a basis to now give them 'both barrels' about all the things they have been doing which have been bugging us! If we do, this will surely be a recipe for disaster.

CHAPTER 12

Confronting Difficult Issues

Confronting difficult issues is a core problem for many Christian organisations. Time and again people have related to me stories where we have been very poor at this and have ducked tackling such issues. The most difficult issues are people problems and for a whole series of reasons we often side-step these challenges. This can be because they are tough, we don't know what to do, we know they will be emotionally draining, we don't want to hurt someone's feelings, or we don't want to get hurt ourselves. Given all of this, what example did Jesus set in this regard?

Firstly, Jesus taught that the difficult should be confronted. In Matthew 5:23-24 he says that if there is something not right between you and your brother, go and resolve it before you make any offering.

In Luke 6:7 we see that the Pharisees and teachers of the law are looking to entrap Jesus. They wanted to see if he would heal on the Sabbath, believing that if he did then he would have contravened the rules of his day. Jesus knows what they are thinking and confronts them by saying in Luke 6:9, 'I ask you which is lawful on the Sabbath: to do good or to do evil, to save life or to destroy it?' They have no answer to this apart from to fume and scheme amongst themselves. Here Jesus sees thinking and practice which is a distortion of the truth and confronts it verbally and then tangibly as he heals the man with the shrivelled hand on the Sabbath, in front of these same Pharisees and teachers of the law.

In John 2:14-16, Jesus is incensed when he enters the Temple in Jerusalem and he finds people using it as a market. They are selling cattle, sheep, doves and exchanging money. This is a full-blown commercial operation in action. Jesus physically confronts this wrongdoing. He makes a whip out of cords and drives all these traders out of the Temple. In John 2:16 he also speaks against this state of affairs saying, 'get these out of here! How dare you turn my Father's house into a market!' As might be expected these actions did not make him popular with all those who were there and many demanded to know by what authority he acted. Despite the difficulties and the risk he was running, Jesus immediately and clearly confronts and deals with unacceptable behaviour, and the desecration of his Father's house.

Jesus is able to see the motivation of others and this leads him to deal with those who are seeking to trap him or whose motives are suspect. In Mark 12:13-17, the Pharisees and Herodians try to catch Jesus out by asking him if taxes should be paid to Caesar or not. They wrap the question up with flattery but their intent is clear; they think if Jesus says do not pay Caesar he will be promoting law breaking and will be in danger from the Roman authorities, and if he says the tax should be paid, he will be unpopular with the Jewish people for supporting an unpopular new tax. Jesus confronts this malicious attempt to trap him by answering, 'give to Caesar what is Caesar's and to God what is God's.' His answer confronts the difficult, and is not easy for the hearers. He is telling the Jews that taxes should be paid, and that we need to honour temporal authority. To the Romans, he is distinguishing Caeser from God, and is saying Caesar is not God, as they promoted. For all hearers he is challenging them to fully honour God.

Here he is tough and confronts the difficult. It is useful to contrast this with the passage later in Mark 12:28-34 where, when asked a genuine question, Jesus gives a full and enlightening answer—explaining which is the greatest and second greatest commandment.

Jesus does not limit this confrontation to his opponents and he is also prepared to confront his own disciples. In Mark 8:33 he rebukes Peter saying, 'get behind me, Satan!' Jesus has been teaching the disciples that he will be rejected, suffer and be killed. Peter does not like this teaching and decides to take Jesus to one side to rebuke him. This is not Peter's idea of what should happen to the Messiah and he wants to set Jesus straight on this. His intervention elicits the above response from Jesus who goes on to say in Mark 8:33, 'you (Peter) do not have in mind the things of God, but the things of men!' Again we see Jesus is willing to confront wrong thinking in a clear and even harsh way.

John14:9 shows us that he is also not afraid to confront one of his own disciples who cannot see the truth. Jesus is talking to the disciples about the fact that he is the way to God, and that he is one with God the Father. Philip does not get this and says to Jesus, look just show us the Father and then we'll be satisfied, that's all we need. Jesus is exasperated by this remark saying to Philip, 'don't you know me, Philip, even after I have been among you such a long time? Anyone who has seen me has seen the Father. How can you say "Show us the Father?"' Again when people are 'not getting it' and are off course Jesus will confront this, even when the issue exists within his closest circle of followers.

So in the gospels we see that a willingness to confront the difficult is demonstrated, and through the model of Jesus we are taught that we should take on things that are wrong. The proviso to this seems to be that this confrontation must be done in the right way. In Matthew 18:15–18 Jesus lays down a methodology for confronting the difficult and seeing an issue through.

In this passage we see that if we have a problem with another person that we should seek to resolve this with them in the first instance. If they won't listen then we should involve other, selected people. If this does not work, we should take it to the full body and if this does not work we should employ sanctions, including expulsion. This formula is easy to write down but I expect many of us would find this pretty difficult to carry out in our own organisations. Having said this, this is the model that we are given and not only this but we can also see that Jesus was willing to confront the unacceptable.

I think we need to be prepared to tackle the difficult and in the gospel we have another clue for doing this effectively. This is that Jesus' willingness to confront the difficult is also married to the value he places on people and the love he has for them. In Matthew 10:29-31 he talks about the enormous value God places on people and their importance to him. He talks of how God knows and values everything about us, he even knows the number of hairs on our head. In Mark 2:17, after calling Levi the tax collector to be a follower, Jesus talks of his mission. Here he explains that, 'it is not the healthy who need a doctor, but the sick. I have not come to call the righteous, but sinners.' He shows how he values all people no matter their (sinful) condition, and that his ministry is focused on saving the lost, and not only those who are already saved.

In Luke 6:27-31 Jesus calls on us all to mirror the value he places on people. He tells us of the need to treat others (even our enemies!) well. In fact he says we should treat them as well we would treat ourselves! We also see the enormous value which Jesus places on people when, in John 15:15, we see he values the disciples as friends and not as servants. The Son of God offers them friendship and equality!

Here again we seem to have a perfect model for our own organisations and our own relationships. We should be prepared to confront the difficult, we should not allow issues to go unattended, and we should tackle things that are not right. In doing this, we need to start from a place where we value people. We will then be able to address poor performance, unacceptable standards, and relationships that are not right: we will be motivated to approach them from the stance of seeking to resolve them for the benefit of the person or group involved, as well as for the entire organisation.

CHAPTER 13

Humility and Resolve

PERSONAL HUMILITY COUPLED with a high resolve to achieve the mission of the organisation is a mighty combination, and a combination we still seek in great leaders today. This combination is described as the highest form of organisational leadership in Jim Collins's book *Good to Great* and is labelled *level 5 leadership*. It's the kind of leadership that builds great organisations, and organisations that will last over the long haul.

In Matthew 18:4 Jesus teaches that whoever humbles himself like a child will be the greatest in the Kingdom of Heaven, and later in Matthew 20:26-28 he says that whoever wants to be great must be a servant or even a slave. In Mark 10:45 he makes it clear that, 'the Son of Man did not come to be served, but to serve.' Then in John 13:4-5 we are given the incredible picture of Jesus washing the feet of his disciples, a task normally reserved for a servant. The last supper is about to be served, Jesus knows that he will soon be facing his greatest test and that Judas has already betrayed him. There is no one to wash the feet of the diners, and Jesus steps forward and, wrapping a towel around his waist, he pours water into a basin and begins to wash the feet of the disciples. Peter is scandalised that his Lord should take on this menial task. He says he will never let Jesus wash his feet, Jesus says he must accept this or he will have no real unity with his Lord. The feet washing is an example to the disciples. It models that they must be servant leaders, leading with humility and being prepared to put others first.

So, there is little doubt about Jesus' humility, but what about his resolve? We see this in many places and perhaps most clearly in Jesus' resolve to complete his mission. He has come from heaven to save humanity from its sins. Jesus' commitment to this mission is such that he is prepared to give his own life to accomplish this task. He takes on God's judgement, a judgement that we should rightly bear, and pays for the price of this judgement by dying on the cross. The sinless man takes on the sins of the world, and so fulfils God's rescue plan for humanity.

It is harder to find greater resolve than this, and we see him saying to Peter in John 16:23 that no one will distract him from what he has to do. In Mark 14:36 we see him in Gethsemane, knowing what he will experience but again committing himself to the Father's will. He goes on to fulfil this will even though it means pain, degradation, suffering and death. This is real resolve! It is also another example for us, an example of exemplary leadership. From this example we can see that the leader maintains a personal humility, but does not get distracted from achieving what he and 'the organisation' has to achieve. If the vision and mission has been set correctly, then the leadership should show resolve and stay on course to fulfil it. In so doing they should ask others to also commit themselves to the goal, and to use their energy and talents to deliver it.

CHAPTER 14

Personal Responsibility

Jesus provides many examples of how leaders should behave and what should be expected of them and of the people they lead. Jesus also provides a further message *for the led* and that is we all have a personal responsibility for how we respond to circumstance and messages. We all know that we will encounter many situations, these are often unexpected and we cannot control them. All we can control is how we react to them, and here we do have a choice.

Consider something simple like a traffic-jam on the way home from work, something we have probably all experienced! We cannot control when the jam happens and how long it lasts, but we can control our response to this situation. At one end of the spectrum we can quickly become frustrated by it, fuming at the inconvenience and lost time, and shouting at the incompetence of other drivers. We can wind ourselves up into a bad mood and then carry this bad mood into our home, ruining our family's evening in the process. Alternatively we can accept that there is little that can be done about the jam and we can relax, put the radio on, catch up on some CDs we want to hear, maybe play a sermon pod cast, pray, or take this as an opportunity for some thinking time. We can arrive home calm and can spread this mood throughout the house—two very different outcomes to the same set of circumstances!

Similarly, God has given us the free will to decide how we respond to the 'truths' presented to us. This is a small thing to say and a huge thing for each of our lives. People may well become locked into a life of misery and repetition of previous problems by a belief that the response to these things is to believe that they are inevitable, somehow legitimate and will be repeated. Many people who abuse others have been themselves the victims of abuse, many women who are abused return to their abuser, and many young offenders repeat their offence within 2 years. People can become locked into a negative cycle by their response to it. Similarly, people can become liberated by their response to what they hear and see around them.

This requires us all to take personal responsibility for the response we make. In Mark 4:1-8 we read the parable of the sower—this is a familiar story in which the farmer (God) scatters his seed (the word) to the world. People then react in different ways; some are so sinful they don't even hear it properly, some hear it and are full of joy but have no staying power and soon give up on the word, some hear the word but allow life's problems to distract them, and some hear the word and accept it and live their lives accordingly. The outcome here is not governed by the gift but by how people respond to it. We are called to make the right response and to take personal responsibility for this response.

This message is echoed in Luke 14:16-21, the parable of the great banquet. A man prepares a great banquet and sends his servant to tell those who had been invited. However, they all start making excuses, one has bought a new field and wants to spend time with his new possession, another has just bought some oxen and wants to try them out and one has just got married. The servant reports to the master that they are not coming and the master sends him out into the streets and alleys to bring the crippled, the blind and the lame to the banquet. He also orders that none who were originally invited will get a taste of the banquet. Here God issues an invitation to enter into His house, an invitation that is extended to us again and again. Many times people refuse this because they are *too busy*. Eventually it will be too late to accept the invitation. Here again we must take personal responsibility for our response to God's word and to His invitation.

In the story of the Syro-Phoenician woman, in Mark 7:26-39, we also see how a faithful response is honoured. The woman has a sick daughter she goes and pleads with Jesus for his help. She is a Greek, born in Syrian Phoenicia, and Jesus offers her a challenging reply that he came to feed the Jews and not waste his ministry on foreigners. In Mark 7:27 he says, 'first let the children eat all they want for it is not right to take the children's bread and toss it to their dogs.' A pretty challenging response to her request! Undeterred, the woman responds by demonstrating her faith; all she needs is the smallest morsel of God's word saying, 'yes, Lord, but even the dogs under the table eat the children's crumbs.' Jesus is pleased and impressed with her response. In return he cures her daughter.

Wherever we are in our organisations, and whatever position we occupy, we have a personal responsibility for our own response to the events and teaching around us. We can often choose to be faithful and respond positively or to be headstrong and respond negatively. Normally our response has consequences for those around us. Positivity often breeds positivity and similarly negativity breeds negativity. So a part of how our organisation is, and how it behaves, is down to how we decide to respond to teaching and events, and how we decide to exercise our personal responsibility.

In this area, leaders may carry an additional personal responsibility—that is to make the right response to followers and to care for them. In Mark 12:28-34 Jesus is asked a genuine question by one of the teachers of the law, this man asks, 'of all the commandments, which is the most important?' Seeing this is a genuine question, Jesus gives the answer, 'the most important commandment is 'Love the Lord your God with all your heart and with all your soul and with all your mind and with all your strength. The second is this: Love your neighbour as yourself.' There is no commandment greater than these.'

Here the man asking the question gets a full and enlightening response, which he acknowledges is helpful to him, and on which he comments, showing he really understands the implications of the answer. Jesus then offers him further encouragement saying, 'you are not far from the kingdom of God.' So the leader, in addition to their own personal response to teaching and circumstances, must also make the right response for their followers—caring for them and enlightening them where possible.

PART THREE

CHAPTER 15

The Interviews

So far we have talked about the challenges that Christian organisations face in dealing with the people issues, and the model we can find in scripture to help us address these issues. More specifically, we looked at Jesus' interactions with others to help us understand how we should behave and what might help us tackle the people part of our organisations better.

I now want to continue to look at the positive things we can do to manage people issues, and I want to do this by drawing on current good practice. As I said earlier, I was honoured to talk to many people in the course of researching this book. These people were not only kind enough to discuss the challenges they faced in people interactions, but they also outlined the many positive courses of action open to Christian bodies. The people I talked to were all committed Christians; some are running churches, others are running charities, others are giving consultancy to Christian bodies, and some are Christian lay leaders with extensive business experience.

The interviews, in order of discussion, were held with:

Chris Edwards—Pastor (Australia)
Roger Morgan—Christian Charity Leader (UK/US)
Jill Garret—Consultant & Thought Leader (UK)
Adam Isaacs—Political Professional (European Parliament)
David Kratt—Theological College, Marketing Director (UK)
Richard Parrish—Head Teacher (UK)
Nigel Tween—Academic (UK)
Andrew Wooding Jones—Director, Christian Centre (UK)
Jill Garfitt—Christian Charity Leadership Team Member (UK)
Chris Start—Businessman and Christian Charity Board Member (UK)
Fraser Bell—Recruiter (UK)
John Hollows—Businessman & Church Elder (UK/Europe)
Karen Brown—Businesswoman and Christian Charity Board Chair (UK)
Mike Fowles—Businessman & Church Elder (UK/Europe)
Ann Start—HR Manager Christian Charity (UK)
Sammy Mah—Christian Charity Leader (US)
Dave Travis—Christian Charity Leader (US)
Jeff Rutt—Founder and Christian Charity Leader (US)
Robert Newhouse—Former Businessman and Church Business Manager (UK)
Matthew Frost—Christian Charity Leader (UK)
Paul Valler—Author and Consultant (UK)

Peter Greer—Christian Charity Leader (US)
John Walker—Businessman & Church Elder (UK)
Robert Lewis—Pastor (US)
Bill Hann & Byron Davis—Executive Pastors (US)
Rich Stearns—Christian Charity Leader (US)
Alan Johnson—Christian Charity Leader (UK)
Fred Pink—Consultant (UK)
Glen Davies—Bishop (Australia)
Kate Marshall—Consultant (UK)
Paul Harrington—Pastor (Australia)
Nick Baines—Bishop (UK)
Rebecca Rumsey—Consultant (UK)
Philip Mountstephen—Pastor (UK/Europe)
Steve Chalk—Christian Charity Leader (UK)
Tim Thornton—Bishop (UK)

In this next section I shall be drawing extensively on their input and experience as we consider what good practice exists around us today and what the kind of things we can adopt that will help us manage people issues effectively. Clearly, not all solutions will apply in all circumstances and some of the things outlined in the following chapters may not be of value to you or your organisation. However, I offer them as food for thought and encouragement from others in the field. Of course, many activities are common sense and some are easy to outline and hard to apply in practice. Despite this, there do seem to be many good things that we can use to help ensure that we build truly effective organisations that, above all, honour God. Like many things, getting the people part of our organisations right seems to start with establishing firm foundations from the 'get go'.

CHAPTER 16

Get Aligned

Alignment

WE TALKED A lot in the first part of the book about the challenges of not being aligned and how this can divide an organisation and reduce its effectiveness. If an organisation wants to be successful then one of the most important things it can do is to get aligned, and ensure that it is properly grounded. One of my interviewees, Richard Parrish, really helped to unpack this. He explained that this grounding and alignment really had to be a deep, and not superficial, thing. Alignment is not only about common purpose, he explained, but also about strong relationships where all parts of the organisation are fully connected. This includes the leadership, who will understand what all parts of the organisation are really thinking. Grounding takes several aspects; let's take a look at these together in the followings sections.

A shared vision

It seems to be universally true that effective organisations have clear visions. They have a common understanding of their purpose and goals. This vision is clearly articulated and bought into by all the membership, not only by the leadership or a small group. This creates a real sense of common ownership and enables everyone to understand where the organisation is headed and what it is trying to achieve. It is also really empowering, as people intuitively understand what the organisation is trying to achieve and how they can best serve the mission.

This clarity of vision not only releases huge energy, as everyone knows what they are about and what they are seeking to do, it also helps the organisation to stick to its chosen course. A shared vision has another really important benefit, and that is it allows people to decide if this is the body they want to be part of, or if they should serve elsewhere.

On this latter point, as we are all grown ups with our own thinking, it is of course right that not everyone will feel motivated or called to serve in every organisation. Some bodies are a good fit for some people, and some are not. Clarity of vision allows people to make a choice, a choice that is helpful, and healthy, not only for the organisation but also for the people themselves. Many good organisations spend a lot of time explaining to potential new members what they are about and how they do things, so that people can decide if this is the right place for them. This seems to be fair to both parties and also gives a reference point if people and the organisation diverge at a later stage. In this circumstance you can measure who has moved, is it the organisation or you?

Let's take an example. One of the organisations I talked with for this book was Hope International. This charity is a Christian micro-finance organisation operating in Africa, Asia, the Ukraine, and other parts of the developing world. Hope is based in Pennsylvania and has enjoyed a high level of clarity about its mission from day one. It seeks to alleviate poverty by making small loans to groups of individuals. These loans enable the people who receive them to break free from the worst forms of poverty by establishing or growing their own businesses. The loan must be repaid, no collateral is needed but the loans are made to individuals in groups, the membership of which they select themselves. If a loan is not re-paid the next person in the group is unable to benefit from a loan. Repayment rates are almost 100%. The loans are often small by western standards; $50, $100 or a couple of hundred dollars, but they are transformational in material terms for the recipients and their families. They also confer dignity in that the individuals raise themselves up with the help of a loan. They do not receive a hand-out and do not fall into dependency on others. This provision of loans, however, is only part of the Hope story; the other part is that from the outset the organisation decided it not only wanted to transform lives physically in tough places, but also wanted to transform them spiritually as well. Because of this, their loan officers are Christians, and with the loans come bible teaching and exploration, and teaching on good Christian business practice. All activities are covered in prayer.

Let's consider for a moment the power of having, and sticking to, this clear vision. The vision *transforming lives physically and spiritually in tough places* is at the core of Hope. It means that it is clear to their associates, volunteers, and those receiving loans what they are signing up for. It is clear that micro-financing and propagation of the gospel are two sides of the same coin for Hope. It's clear that this is not just another micro-finance organisation, or a charity that only wants to provide material relief. In the latter case, people wanting to make a positive contribution in tough places on humanitarian grounds know that to serve with this organisation they also need to embrace Christianity and the furtherance of the gospel. If they can't do this then Hope is not for them, and they should seek to utilise their talents in a different organisation.

This clarity not only allows choices to be made, it also gives Hope great coherence and cohesion as an organisation and allows it to pursue its calling to the fullest. It also allows this organisation to stick to its mission and not to deviate from the course that it feels called to follow. This kind of clarity builds strength, credibility and capability as the organisation goes forward.

Doing a few things well

Talking to the interviewees, it became clear that really effective organisations not only have a clear vision, they also seek to ensure that they have a set of goals which clearly support the vision. They also seek to deliver the vision by pursuing a *few* carefully chosen goals. In other words they seek *to do a few things well* and do not aim to try and do everything. This focus means that they enjoy a high degree of success as resources are concentrated on winning in a few areas and are not dissipated by trying to do lots of things. This means they avoid getting side tracked by things that sometimes have little relationship either to one another or to the vision.

In this regard, consider the top sports person. Generally, if a person wants to excel as a tennis player, golfer, or soccer star they need to focus on their sport from an early age. They then need to retain this focus as they train to make their dreams a reality. As they operate in highly competitive environments, they know that to be successful they must develop their talent and skill to the highest level they can. In tennis the difference between the world's no. 1 and no. 50 is a small margin, it's not a gaping chasm, so success means being focused and highly disciplined in one's field.

This idea of having a clear vision and then pursuing it with a few key goals also seems to apply to effective Christian organisations. Take the example of Willow Creek. This church has grown and prospered because from its outset there was a clear understanding that they were focused on reaching the un-churched for Jesus Christ. They did not dilute this and seek other groups, they stuck with this focus, building new techniques and methodologies, but all of them focused on achieving this goal.

Rick Warren talks about the need for having a specific purpose in church building. He says 'a narrow mission is a clear mission' and quotes the Salvations Army's original mission to, 'make citizens of the rejected' to illustrate his point. Warren talks about how the vague mission statement has little impact and urges people to develop specific purpose statements that can focus energy and ensure you don't get diverted on peripheral issues. He ends with a great question, 'what are the very few things that will make the most difference for Jesus' sake in our world?'

Contrast this with many churches we see where ministries grow up dependent on the passion and enthusiasm of members. Different members have different passions so many different ministries grow up. The original intention of the church then becomes submerged under all these conflicting and unaligned activities. The church had originally intended to head left, but now it's heading right, left, straight ahead and the rest! This unaligned and multiple approach tends to dissipate the effectiveness of the organisation and means it is never really focused enough to achieve high standards and high levels of success.

Grounding character

Great organisations not only have a clearly understood and supported vision, and a focused set of goals that support this vision, they also have a well-grounded set of *values*. These values provide the character of the organisation, they speak to 'how things will be done around here'. They allow a person to know how they will be valued and how they should value others. They explain to the leaders what is expected of them, and what behaviour is required by the organisation.

For these values to be fully grounded and adhered to, they normally have to fulfil three criteria. Firstly, they have to be *healthy* things we want to promote; e.g. relationships that are real and supportive and leaders who are truly connected to the organisation. Secondly, they have to be stated so all can read them and understand them. It's hard to buy into something that is not clear. Thirdly, they have to be lived out or they are not really worth anything and will not form the character of the organisation and become part of its DNA.

Values are not abstract ideas that are only interesting at a theoretical level. It is highly likely that your individual values and beliefs *will shape your behaviour*. They will actually determine who you are and how you relate to others.

Let me given an example of this. Many years ago I used to have a boss who did not much value social interaction—he loved business interactions and discussion, but not social ones. As a consequence, he would often enter the offices without looking left or right, and offered no greetings or small talk on the way to his own room. This behaviour did not seem in the least odd to him. He was not trying to ignore anyone or send any negative messages. He just did not have a need to interact with others socially, and so did not spend time on this. Now, as you might expect his behaviour did send messages. Inadvertently, he was making people feel that they were being deliberately snubbed and that they were not being acknowledged because they had done something wrong. Once this behaviour, and its consequences, was pointed out to the boss he was mortified and worked hard to correct it.

Contrast this to a person who loves interaction and naturally values people. She is likely to spend time on the way to her own office acknowledging people, catching up, asking them to come by and give her ideas on the latest project and the like. These two very different behaviours are driven by values and beliefs.

In organisations, the behaviour of the organisation is also linked to the values of the body and the culture this generates. Values are therefore important and it's worth spending time agreeing these values and working out what how you will apply them in practice. This is not only going to have a huge influence in aligning behaviour and increasing effectiveness; it's also going to govern how we treat each other. Great values will lead to an effective organisation and a great environment for its people.

Theological grounding

Christian organisations also need to agree their central theology to be effective. There are theological questions that are open to interpretation and can be debated. This, in turn, can lead organisations to be debilitated by endless internal debate. In these debates passions are likely to run high. These matters are part of faith and people feel they can not, and should not, compromise on their beliefs. A failure to resolve these issues can rob an organisation of any real chance of effectiveness. Vast amounts of the organisation's energy starts to be poured into internal debate (and argument) and not into focusing on and achieving its mission.

This is a tough challenge, and one that besets many organisations. We only have to look at the debate rumbling on in the Church of England over the centrality of scripture and what the church's approach should be to homosexuality.

In terms of looking at how the issue of theological grounding might be addressed, I am grateful to Matthew Frost the CEO of Tearfund. This is a leading UK based Christian charity, working through local churches to alleviate physical poverty and to promote spiritual growth. Matthew suggested that of course organisations must be clear as to their theological position. However, given the complexity of this subject, they should also be careful to limit the theological issues to the ones that they see as key to their situation. The organisation may not have a view on every theological issue, indeed it may prove impossible to do so. They should however decide what is core for them, and then should maintain a very clear stance on these fundamentals. In addition to this, we need to be sure that we have access to good scholarship and able scholars who can help us understand and interpret issues as they arise.

Having a clear theological grounding should not be ducked. Indeed it should be used positively to give substance and character to the organisation. If the organisation is bible believing, and sees the bible as the revealed word of God, a revealed word that is not limited by historical context, then it needs to be clear on this. This should be part of the foundation of the organisation. Conversely, if the organisation wants to promote the role of women and have them occupy leadership roles, then it needs to be clear on its theology in this regard. It needs to say and show that for them male headship is not a core issue for the organisation.

Critical mass

It seems that where organisations can embrace or develop a clear vision and develop a limited number of effective goals to support this vision, then it is likely to flourish. To get to this point takes hard work, and this may be trickier to achieve if you have an existing organisation than when you're establishing a new one. However, even in existing organisations, you're unlikely to break free of the *gravity* created by multiple agendas and a lack of focus unless you are able to make this change.

Inheriting an existing organisation can be tough. It might well be divided, faction ridden, or bound by past practices and stuck in its ways. There may be little apparent willingness to change even though the organisation is not successful. To change this will take hard work, but the leader can start by casting a compelling vision. This vision has to be explained and communicated widely, and the way of achieving it needs to be made clear.

The leader has to use this vision to find allies who want to change, both from within the existing organisation (they will be there) and from outside. He or she then has to keep building until a critical mass of people buy into the vision and are committed to living it out and bringing it about. This critical mass will generate their own momentum and others will join. If the course of action is healthy, the leader committed enough, and critical mass attained, then the vision is likely to be delivered.

Clearly, in this model some will leave the boat. They will not be happy that change is taking place, and will not be able to accept this change. In this case let them leave as graciously as possible, and pray that they will find a place that is right for them. Some may not leave voluntarily and may seek to stay to fight the changes. Well, here we are back to confronting the difficult; if people don't want to buy in and embrace the new direction them sometimes you will have to ask them to leave. It will be best for the organisation and probably best for them.

The body

In 1 Cor 12:12 we're told that the body is made up of many parts. Each of these parts has a unique function, but all have value and all are part of the *same body*.

This is a good analogy for an aligned and grounded organisation. Clear vision, goals and roles give us a real opportunity to work effectively together to achieve a common aim. Like the parts of the body, we may all have different roles. One may be the visionary leader (the eyes) another may be the practical doer (the hands) and another may carry the administrative burden (the feet). However, all are needed to make the body function effectively. They all need to work together in a common cause and direction if the whole body is going to get to where it wants to be!

This analogy of the body is also helpful in showing that alignment can also allow for individual participation to flourish. Alignment should not be a 'straight jacket' that prevents individual thinking and talents to be used. Rather, alignment should be liberating and empowering for individual contributions. By having a clear direction, people should be able to see how they can use their talents to assist in achieving the vision and goals of the organisation. It should also allow for individual innovation as people see how they and the organisation can do things differently and better in order to achieve its mission. This chimes in with the idea that good empowerment is liberating—it gives clear direction and a framework but allows people to be innovative and flexible in reaching the goals.

How can I apply this?

If you want to harness the power of alignment as a leader then there are some clear things that you must do.

- Firstly you must develop **a compelling vision**, be prepared to cast this vision and then reinforce it time and time again. Remember Bill Hybels describes a vision as *a picture of the future that produces passion today*. This picture does not have to be developed by a leader alone, in fact it's better if the leadership team develop this together. People have a higher 'buy-in' to things that they have had a hand in developing. However, the leader needs to own the direction of this vision and have some thoughts as to what s/he want it to be—a leader cannot be passive in this process.
- This vision needs to be clear, i.e. it needs to **give clarity about the direction and the goal**, it needs to show what are the key priorities for the organisation, it needs to help clarify what you won't do, and it should be guide the

organisation's objectives, and the objectives of individuals within the organisation.

- People, both staff and volunteers, should be **held accountable against the objectives which the vision requires**, and the leadership needs to be honest about expectations of what has to be done and how it has to be done.

- Through healthy relationships leaders should promote vision and alignment. **Go beyond nice and show you really value people by dealing with them adult to adult.** Apply this in explaining the direction the vision requires, the few things the organisation will focus on, the accountability needed and the things that the organisation will *not* be focusing on.

- Enhance alignment by your own behaviour as a leader. **Be authentic in acknowledging and tackling difficult issues**, state risks and frame choices about the future, show humility and resolve. Through your own behaviour e.g. being really interested in others, elicit the response and support you seek.

- Underpin this alignment of vision and action with an alignment of values. **Be clear as to the values you want to see promoted** e.g. integrity and trust, commitment to working through others, 'we go' not 'I go', and being accountable.

CHAPTER 17

Healthy Relationships

In Acts 2 the church is depicted as having the most caring and supportive community imaginable, it's a place where people come together on equal terms and support and love each other. This support takes on a tangible form as the richer members sell their goods to support those who are less well off. This picture of community once again shows the centrality of relationships in the Christian world. We not only value relationships but are also called to live in real fellowship with one another.

The right attitude

Given the importance of relationships, then, it's important that we have the right attitude to these, and seek to ensure that they are healthy.

We have to value each other, and to value each other enough that we will seek grown up, adult-to-adult relationships where we can be real, open and honest. We need to build communities where we can 'speak the truth in love' and where people know that we start from a point where we value and love them. Because of this, we will be able to be clear and honest with them if their behaviour is unacceptable, or if there is an issue with how they relate to the community or perform their role. We talked earlier about how it is not respectful to treat other adults as children. This tends to show that we value them less than ourselves. Real respect calls for real relationships, which are grounded in love and capable of addressing difficult issues when the need arises.

To really get grounded we do have to face some *personal challenges*. Challenges like seeking to love the people we are in community with. This need applies to all of us and is especially important in leaders as they set the standards for others. If they love the people, they have a wonderful chance of having great relationships and building great communities. It is of course tough to love all of the people we interact with in our Christian organisations, but we should seek to start from this point, and to pray a lot about it!

If we can try to do this, relationships will be strong, people will know we want the best for them and when there is disagreement people will also know that they are still valued. They will know that any disagreement is about behaviour or about the specific issue being debated, and it's not about who they are. There's a soccer analogy that says that when you tackle someone, you should *go for the ball not the man* i.e. tackle the issue or the behaviour, not the character of the person. Too often we see issues becoming personalised, and once this happens they are likely to escalate out of all proportion and, even when resolved, a bitter taste is often left behind for all parties.

Parent/child relationships

We talked in an earlier chapter about how adopting parent/child relationships within our organisations can stand in the way of the development of healthy relationships. There is a helpful story in Jamie and Maren Showkeir's book *Authentic Conversations* which illustrates the value of moving to adult-to-adult conversations if we are to build real and valuable relationships. The Showkeirs tell the story of Joe, an executive of a failing newspaper who called them in for advice and consultation. The paper was in trouble and all the staff knew this. Joe spent all his day reassuring staff and telling them not to worry, that he and the senior management would keep them safe and fix the problems which the business faced.

Joe was a bright and capable man, with a real passion for his job and he was committed to his employees. He wanted to do the right thing in trying to reassure them, but in effect he was treating them like kids. They knew that all was not well, that the paper was in real trouble. They also knew that he was trying to reassure them but thought that he was not being straight with them. In fact he was making the situation worse by making promises he could not keep and sending a message to the employees that they were 'off the hook' for resolving the difficult situation the paper faced. Ironically, he was exacerbating the problem the business was facing!

The Showkeirs talked to Joe and explained to him that this parent to child approach was not helping and in fact it was destructive. Joe thought over their input and recognised the truth of it. He then called an 'all hands' meeting and addressed the workforce. He decided to take what seems to be a high risk strategy and explained to them clearly and directly the full gravity of the situation. He decided to explain the challenge that the paper faced in becoming profitable in the market. He talked to the employees, outlining the situation and admitting that he had made it worse by telling them that he and the senior team had the answers to the difficulties that lay ahead, and by reassuring employees that they would be all right when he could not be sure of this. He was clear about the costs of failure and said he needed everyone to begin taking responsibility for finding the answers. He was emphatic that everyone would need to work together to turn the organisation around. He also said that he could not do anything about their current unhappiness. It was in their hands how they reacted to the situation and they had to choose for themselves how they handled the future. He would do all he could to save the paper but they had to decide now how they responded to this challenge.

Having taken this approach Joe waited with baited breath for the reaction. The reaction was that, after a moment, the employees spontaneously stood up and applauded—for a long time. They had been told the truth for the first time in years and Joe had acknowledged that they were adults capable of making up their own minds. He made it clear that he could not resolve the paper's problems by himself, and decided that he needed to be straight with the people whose future was on the line. This was a great moment for the organisation!

How are we behaving?

So, let's have real relationships with each other, relationships which are founded in love and are prepared to be open, honest and grown up.

We instinctively know these things are healthy and will in turn help us build a healthy community and a healthy organisation. If relationships are hard going, we should always start by trying to make a positive change to our own behaviour. This change is likely to bring about a positive change in how others react to us. People will react to our behaviour; if this is positive then the dynamics with those around us are likely to be positive. If we wait for everyone else to change before we're willing to build the right relationship with them, then we're likely to be waiting a long time!

Moreover, we need to be careful that we are not blind to the impact we're having on others. The bible says we reap what we sow and, in relational terms, the attitude we project to a person is likely to be reflected back to us. If we're naturally open with them, clearly value them and like them, then this is the reaction we're likely to get back in return. If, however, we're suspicious, negative or even hostile then we're likely to find that negativity, suspicion and hostility is the response we get.

I have a good friend who radiates fun and openness to people. He values those he meets and communicates this in many ways. He delights at encountering someone new and his hope that a great friendship will develop. Unsurprisingly, people react very positively to him, they like being around him, and want to include him in their activities. They know he's not good at doing all things, and they are sometimes frustrated with some of his actions. Nevertheless, this does not dent the goodwill that exists for him, so when he is in trouble or needs help, people are very willing to step in.

Similarly, we can also unintentionally generate a lot of negatives that affect our relationships. I have another friend who told me that he had a problem with one of his subordinates, a warehouse manager. This problem had gone on for most of his career. My friend's retirement was looming and he decided that he wanted to resolve this relational issue with the manager before he finally retired. He valued the man's capability, although the chemistry between them was poor. On his next visit he resolved to change their normal interaction and to start by telling the person how much he actually valued what he was doing, and how he wanted him to know this before he retired. He also decided to take a new view of the person, and to let go many of the negative assumptions he had made about him.

During his next visit to the warehouse he started to talk positively about the manager's contribution and warmed to his theme as time went on. As he spoke, he could see the barriers coming down and felt the man listening to him. He finished speaking realising that this new approach had helped, but he was still surprised when the manager said 'thanks for saying that and do you know that this is the first time I feel that I can speak to you properly and have a real conversation with you.'

From there they broke the ice and their relationship started out on a new footing. The point of this story is not only that we reap what we sow, and that sometimes this can be more negative than we wanted, but also to say that we can sometimes waste decades in misunderstanding each other! This is a pretty big waste of time and energy by anyone's yardstick.

Be, do, get

Penny Ferguson, the personal leadership guru, expounds a very helpful practice in building good relationships. This theory, which is borne out by practice, is described as BE, DO, GET. By changing *how we are* with people, for example being more open, trusting, appreciative, calm, positive, relaxed and so on. Then by changing what we do; listening more, keeping our mouths shut, looking for the positives in people, and seeking their views. We can get a much better and more helpful relationship with them; this is not a trick, but a desire to value people more and relate to them better. I have seen this work and have heard its effects described many times. The effects of very small changes in behaviour can be enormous.

Just think if you're a leader who never really spends time getting to know your team, think what you're communicating to them about how you value them. They probably think that you're not interested in them and that they are only tools for doing the job. Think now about the effect you could have if you were to find time getting to know them and seeking out their ideas and inputs. The change is likely to be remarkable. If this change is to work properly then it has to be sustained and genuine, people can smell phoney behaviour from a hundred miles.

Character and persona

If we want to relate to people in a genuine manner then it's better to relate to them from our real character. This means relating from who we truly are, rather than from some persona (who we feel we need to be) that we have adopted. People who relate from character have a real chance of being authentic, trusting, compassionate, courageous, and confident. Those coming from a persona can be image conscious, controlling, self interested, uneasy, self centred and false. Our relationships gain real power from being natural and open.

This chapter is a call for us to value each other highly and, because of this, to have genuine and real relationships with each other. Just think about the strength your community would gain if this were the norm. In this circumstance, difficult issues can be tackled without the person being destroyed. It can be accepted that people are loved and valued and that issues will be tackled in this context; and because people are valued and loved, unacceptable behaviour will be tackled in a grown up, adult-to-adult way. It can also be the norm that we won't ignore problems and we won't try and resolve them with sledgehammer tactics that destroy the person and hurt the organisation.

The cobbler's children

One more thought about relationships in Christian and other not-for-profit bodies that a senior manager working in a charity recently imparted to me. The cause people are working for can be so central and important to them that it overshadows the need to be mindful of people's needs. It can be that because of this, people are expected to give their all to the cause and to subjugate all personal needs.

Well clearly, the work these bodies is engaged in is important, but as well as undertaking this work we must also value people and make sure that their needs for time off, attention, support and so on are also met.

Everyone knows the story of the cobbler's children where the cobbler was so busy providing shoes to other people that he never made any for his own children. In the same way, we must ensure that we're not so busy offering compassion, support and understanding to others that we don't offer this to the people working for us.

How can I apply this?

A key question is 'how can I build healthy relationships in my organisation?' We've considered in this chapter the need for us to value others if we're going to have a positive relationship with them, the need for 'grown up' adult-to-adult relationships, and the need to think about how we're relating to others and what messages we're sending them—both verbally and non-verbally. In addition to this, there is another powerful idea is contained in the book *Authentic Conversations* by Jamie and Maren Showkeir which I quoted earlier.

This idea is that relationships are the result of conversations, and that authentic conversations can help us build the healthy relationships that we are seeking. What are the elements in having an authentic conversation and what steps can we take?

As you would expect, the first step is to take a look at ourselves to ensure that we value the other person enough to start a new conversation with them based on the premise that:

- They are a complex human being and not an object
- We want to hear their views about their individual thoughts and plans and that we don't view these things as useless and irrelevant to the issue in hand
- We will take account of people's freedom and self accountability and not ignore the freedom and will of the individual
- We will present genuine choices as the primary means

of engagement rather than seeking ways of shaping the other person's behaviour

- We will be prepared to engage in collaboration and goodwill rather than trying to enforce our own will on others
- We will try to understand the other person's perspective rather than ignoring this

If we can engage with this positive perspective, we can have a real conversation with the person and if repeated enough times this approach will change the nature of organisation's culture. It should be noted that this kind of change could be tough. Past certainties will disappear and you may feel less 'in control'. However, by taking this approach you will be preparing yourself to be a better listener, and will acknowledge that your own perspective is only one of many legitimate views. In this new conversation we have to face each other without expectation, without defence, and without a series of predictable responses. It sounds scary but is the start of a really grown up relationship.

Carrying these authentic conversations forward there are other things you can do to ensure they are successful. Here are four common elements for these conversations:

- Honestly acknowledge the difficult issues and name the harsh realities—we have to acknowledge reality to be able to deal with unpredictability, anxiety, frustration and cynicism.
- State your own contribution to the difficult issues and acknowledge its harmful effect—by owning this you take responsibilities for your actions and invite others to examine their own contribution to the difficulty; both acts of commission and omission.

- State the risks and acknowledge the difficulties, including the possibility that things might not work out—the truth is we cannot know the future. To pretend we can is both dishonest and demeaning of others. When the future is uncertain and the risks are explicit, we see how vital it is to work together for a solution.

- Frame choices about how you engage the future—ultimately we are all responsible for the choices we make. With regard to relationships, we must all choose to take responsibility for collaborating with each other and for managing our reactions to both successes and disappointments.

This process and route enables us to be authentic with one another. Acknowledging doubt and failure, our own contributions to problems, naming difficulty issues, disclosing our own feelings, taking responsibility for our own reactions, and committing to an action or result, enables us to avoid manipulation and to have a real relationship with another person.

Finally, when in conversation with others, try to be aware of what is really going on. As well as the content of your discussion there will also be a couple of unsaid things which are going on—these include your own emotional response to the issue in hand. This may take the form of you being concerned about loss of control, your own competence, your need for approval and your self-esteem. This emotional response will also be taking place in the person you are talking to and again you need to try and be aware of how they are reacting to the discussion. Learning to be aware of these more hidden factors is going to enable you to better ensure this is a true and honest conversation that both parties have fully engaged in.

Let's take a look now at some of examples of authentic conversations and how they can help in different (and challenging) circumstances.

Facing a difficult issue—as we've already discussed, sooner or later difficult issues need to be addressed. This leaves us all with the fundamental choice about how we engage with such issues. Here's a process for engaging with this authentically and helping to build a healthy relationship with the other party. Start by extending goodwill and then:

- State the reason for the conversation or meeting—be straight, don't beat around the bush too much
- State your intention to resolve the issue or make it work—show that you are committed to finding a solution
- Name the difficult issue clearly and directly, and without judgement—clearly get the issue on the table
- Own your contribution to the difficult issue—be clear about the part you played by commission or omission
- Invite engagement and request help of the other person—show you want this to be worked out together
- Ask for the other person's viewpoint—look for their factual and emotional viewpoint
- Ask the other person how they want to proceed—engage them in the responsibility of finding a solution
- Try and avoid blaming the other person—they are likely to hear criticism much more loudly than all other points, ideally they need to state and own their contribution to the difficult situation

Proposing change—in many Christian communities this can be a tough thing to do as we can be traditional or have a lot of vested interest in maintaining the status-quo. Here's a possible authentic and healthy approach:

- Describe the change you are proposing—be clear so everyone can understand it
- Give the reasons for proposing this change—ideally these should be as tangible and factual as possible
- Outline the difficult issues involved—show you understand these and are not trying to sweep them under the carpet
- Invite and encourage additional reservations—get these issues out and show you're open to them
- Extend understanding and agreement—make sure people know that they have been heard
- Frame the choices you see for proceeding—put options forward
- Ask them to frame the choices they see—invite additional options
- State the choice you will make, or ask the group how it thinks you should proceed, or acknowledge the differences and ask the group what are the next steps for finding a better way to resolve the problem

Renegotiating an established relationship—we talked earlier about how relationships were complex in Christian organisations and sometimes unclear. In view of this we may well need to recalibrate or renegotiate these relationships.

- State the purpose for the conversation as you see it—here be upfront, it's about the relationship
- Name the difficult issues in the relationship—be clear what you're talking about and not talking about

- Ask for their view of these issues and your contributions to creating them—get their input
- Extend understanding and own your contributions—show you've heard them and own your contribution
- Frame the choices for proceeding and ask them to do the same—make and get inputs on the way ahead
- State your wish to create a new set of agreements for this relationship and name them—show you want a better way of working to exist in the future
- Ask for their engagement and commitment—get their sign up to this new way of working
- Negotiate agreement on future steps or seek further opportunities for discussion—either note agreement or agree to meet again to discuss further

CHAPTER 18

Hire Great Leaders

Hiring the best

I USED TO HAVE an Australian boss who had a very simple model for hiring folk, or so he claimed! He used to say that he only really looked at three criteria. Were people humble or arrogant, were they hard working or lazy, and were they smart or dumb?

He said that if you got two out of three from; *humble, hard working* and *smart* you were likely to be on a winner. This is not the most scientific approach, but in its favour this view was many years before *Good to Great* was published and it echoes some of the ideas presented in that book. The *Good to Great* research showed that humility and resolve are the key characteristics of successful leaders, especially leaders who are successful over the long haul. This result was not pre-ordained by Jim Collins and his team, who were genuinely surprised to find that these characteristics were so significant. They had expected instead that they were going to find that big charismatic leaders were the order of the day in successful companies.

I have been hiring people for nearly 25 years and for much of that time these hires have been for key executive roles. In this process, humility and resolve have always been important qualities to me. In addition, I have also always valued smartness. Indeed, a lot of research would point to leaders being able to demonstrate four types of intelligence. These four intelligences seem to be predictors of success in leadership.

The first of these is Political Intelligence, the ability to understand the organisation, its politics, how it (and its networks) work and how to get things done. Next is Intellectual Intelligence, or intellectual horsepower. This is the smartness; if people are bright they tend to be adaptable, able to solve problems and able to grasp the challenges and complexities of an organisation. Next there is Emotional Intelligence, the ability to manage one's own emotions and to understand and relate to the emotions of others. This latter quality has been highlighted as a key issue in being successful in that those with high IQs (intellectual intelligence) can often struggle in leadership and managerial roles if they lack EQ (emotional intelligence) that enables them to bring their intellect to bear on their situation and environment. Finally, we have Social Intelligence, now often defined as having well developed values, beliefs and spiritual grounding. Clearly this is a key element for any Christian leader, but is now being recognised as a key quality for secular leaders if they wish to be truly successful.

The qualities of a Christian leader

So, what qualities should we look for in our Christian leaders?

From the interviews it would seem that the four types of intelligence in the last section and qualities outlined in the rest of this chapter will offer a high chance of success. It's unlikely that anyone person will demonstrate all of these attributes and indeed in any hire you probably will not get

100% of the qualities you want. However, the thing is to be clear which things you *need* and to search hard to ensure you get near to this model.

I said earlier that seasoned recruiters have a saying that runs, 'if in doubt, don't hire', even if you really want to fill the vacancy. It's easy to say this, and when you do most people nod in agreement and yet despite this time and again we see people making hires they are not fully comfortable with, as they feel pressured to fill the post. Well, hiring anyone, and especially hiring a leader, is one of the most crucial things you can do in any organisation. In view of this, it's worth investing whatever it takes in this process in terms of time and energy. If you low ball recruiting, the decision you make will almost certainly to come back to bite you later.

Scripturally grounded

Humility and resolve are clearly key qualities in a leader, but in our context the most important thing is likely to be that our leaders are scripturally grounded. We want people who know and understand the bible and accept its teaching as the roadmap for their lives. This grounding is a requirement that ranks above all others, and we expect to have evidence that a person is Christ centred and lives out Christian truths in their work, friendships and home life.

In a Christian context, the leader is a reference point for others in the community. Much is expected of leaders and we are expected to work under their authority and guidance. They must therefore be grounded in their faith and live out this faith. If not, how will the community be able to effectively anchor itself and live out Christian standards and values?

So, this is our starting point, and assuming that our leaders are grounded in faith, and are role models for the Word, what else should we look for?

Humility and resolve

As has been said, humility and resolve are key qualities to look for in a leader. Let's now look in a little more detail at what we mean by this.

Humility can sometimes be seen as meaning that a person is a little meek and a little weak. It can be seen as meaning that they are some kind of a push over, and that others will easily overrule them. However, we are not using humility here in this context. Rather we mean that people are not hung up on their own egos and projecting a certain persona. These people are at ease with themselves, they are confident enough about who they are not to always have to seek the limelight. They like to encourage and work through others and are happy for others to be credited with success. As well as this, they will often be willing to shoulder the responsibility, *to carry the can*, when things don't go right.

They accept responsibility and model this—and there's a real echo of the cross here where Jesus shouldered the responsibility for all of our guilt and sin. These leaders are *'we go'* people rather than *'I go'* people. Life for them is about the team and the whole community and not their own personal agenda and need for acclamation. They want to achieve things with their teams, and know that if they can harness the energy of a team or community then they are likely to achieve a successful outcome for their organisation.

These people have personal humility but are not a pushover because coupled with this humility is a steely resolve that the organisation will be successful. They are normally 100% committed to the organisation and its aims. They have a clear determination that the organisation will be successful and that this success will continue once they leave. This resolves enables them to cast a compelling and clear vision. It also enables them to be tenacious when the going gets tough, to be consistent, and to confront difficult issues which may derail the organisation and what it's trying to do.

Give and get

In a Christian context we often express this quality of humility as servant leadership. As we saw when we considered Christ's leadership, great leaders command great authority but are willing to serve others. They are prepared to take the last place, and combine their authority with real humility.

In this model, leadership becomes more about *giving* than *getting*, more about passing something on to others rather than getting something back for it. A great leader will understand that the teaching and role modelling he or she presents is not for his or her own benefit or accolade. Indeed to be truly effective, their focus must not be on themselves but on God and those they are working with and serving. They know that they need not worry if their teaching and modelling benefits them and is universally regarded as being very clever. They know it is more important that their work is of benefit to those who are receiving it.

Not only is this true, but the great leader also knows that they cannot control what they get from others. They cannot make people like them, respect them and so on, all they can control is who they are and what they give. However, they also know that if they give well and generously of themselves then people will tend to respond positively. Seek leaders who understand the need to give and not to get.

Consistency

Many organisations have been severely wounded by a lack of consistency. A continual series of changes in direction, priorities and ways of working has often drained their effectiveness and enthusiasm. Compared to this, many great organisations have demonstrated real consistency in their vision and approach. This does not mean that they have ignored the need to change and adapt or have not embraced new techniques and technologies. However, it does mean that they have been consistent in their fundamentals, they have stuck to their core mission and values, they have looked to the long term and not to short term fads.

This kind of consistency and clarity of direction often comes from, and is reinforced by, the leader and leadership. Given this, consistency is a quality to seek in our leaders, indeed this may be even more important in the Christian world than secular organisations. We talked earlier about the fact that in Christian organisations things often take time to achieve. People often have to be persuaded about a course of action, a way of doing things, or about the direction to be followed. They cannot just be told to do something; they have to sign up to it intellectually and emotionally. Given this, consistency in the leader is highly prized, as it is likely to take time to embed a vision, set of values, and practices. Consistency of direction does not mean that the organisation is closed to innovation, but rather that it stays the course and builds upon its success year upon year until it achieves an extremely high degree of effectiveness.

Consistency may also be required of the leader in another way. When a change is needed, to support the core mission of the organisation, then the leader will be required to be consistent and tenacious in driving this through. There will be resistance and change and the leader will need to be able to handle this. He or she will need the energy to communicate the change and to gain support for it. Most people find change tough, it's hard to give up what we're familiar with and have become used to. We tend to like to stick with the status quo if at all possible. If change is needed then the leader is going to need consistency of intent and consistency in managing the execution of the change.

Integrity and trust

Along with humility, resolve and consistency comes integrity. The leader with a clear sense of direction and commitment, who has personal humility, is likely to confront difficult issues. Their clear sense of direction and lack of personal ego mean that they are not afraid of confronting the difficult and also recognise the need to do this in order that the organisation achieves its goals. They will want to take on any challenges that will prevent the organisation operating to the right standards. If a person lacks these qualities, then personal integrity may get shredded as difficult issues are not confronted, unacceptable behaviour flourishes and poor practices are overlooked.

Coupled with integrity we also look to our leaders to generate trust. This trust will mean that we will commit to them and be prepared to follow them. All other qualities—being scripturally grounded, having humility, resolve and consistency—need to be built on this trust. One way in which the leader engenders trust is to demonstrate good judgement and to show that this judgement is based on prayer and seeking God's wisdom.

Working through others

Great leaders also want to achieve things through others, they are not one-man bands, and know the importance of working in a team and empowering others. It is common sense that an organisation is more effective if ten people are committed and engaged on a task than if just one person is. Try building a house on your own, it'll be a pretty daunting task. These kind of leaders also know that people are going to be motivated by being recognised, by being given responsibility, by being involved and listened to and by being given an opportunity to grow through new challenges and tasks.

Involvement combined with listening and appreciation is a mighty tool for building a team, and building team commitment.

Matthew Frost, CEO of Tearfund, gave me a great example of this. He described how at Tearfund the leadership worked together to refine their vision, set their goals, and hammer out what success looked like for them.

This team effort means the final product has a high degree of ownership from the team. It also carries a high level of creativity as different thinking is harnessed by the process. Moreover, it has been tested by the various opinions and experiences present in the team. Not only has a better end product been delivered, but the process of creating this product has also strengthened and enhanced the team. People want to be engaged in the central activities and direction of their organisation. They want to have real buy in and tend not to want to be idle bystanders to the process. Leaders who are able to appreciate and listen to their people will have a great chance of releasing many talents and much energy for the good of the organisation.

As well as involvement, people also seek appreciation and recognition for what they do. They want this to be genuine, but provided that it is they will feel valued and better about themselves. The likelihood is that they will also pass these positive feelings on to others. Appreciation is a free gift, which leaders can give, and at its best it often only takes a few moments and it means a huge amount to the recipient. Some of the best appreciation comes from a short and genuine comment being made at the moment something has been done well.

I know of a church leader who was a great example when it came to appreciation and encouragement. This person reckoned that he sent out about sixty e-mails per week thanking people for their efforts and encouraging them in what they were doing. These notes were not long, but they were specific and heart felt. They maybe took a few hours of his week, but the effect it had in lifting the whole motivation and spirit of the organisation was immense. People felt appreciated and wanted to do more, they also told others how good they felt which spread a feeling of well being and commitment. The leader has a powerful tool at his or her disposal—the tool of genuine appreciation.

Similarly, by good listening, leaders can allow others to develop their own solutions, and can demonstrate support and affirmation for the person. They can unlock problems through greater understanding. A company asked the Penny Ferguson organisation to run a programme in Italy for their CEOs and for their spouses who would be accompanying them.

Penny decided to run an exercise where the CEOs and their spouses were asked to give each other time and space to properly listen to each other. Under the terms of the exercise, each half of the couple was given 3 minutes of *uninterrupted* time. In this time they were able speak, whilst the other person had to listen. Once one of them had taken their turn then they switched around, and the other partner had their turn. They changed back and forth until they both felt that they had fully explored the topic in hand. The exchanges started and gradually the volume in the room built as more and more came pouring out. The exchanges went on for over an hour, and at the end of this time people were invited to share something of their discussions. One woman, who had teenage children, explained tearfully that this was the *first time* she had felt listened to in her entire married life. Another couple explained how they had resolved an issue that they had been skirting around for months and which had gone unsolved.

The power of listening and appreciation is great. Great Christian leaders demonstrate these qualities, as they will start from a point of loving and valuing the people who serve with them. We need to seek out those who can demonstrate these powerful qualities and if we can find and attract them, we're likely to be doing a great service to our organisations.

As part of wanting to involve and work through others, good leaders are good at giving people responsibility. They are generally good judges of people and know who to approach for each given task. They also know how to empower people effectively. A good friend used to say, 'empowerment is not asking someone to roller skate on top of a skyscraper in the dark—if you do this they are likely to stay firmly at the centre and not move.' What he meant by this is that good empowerment is not giving people carte blanch, or mentioning something in the corridor for two minutes and thinking you have now successfully got the person to take on the organisation of the church's week-end away. There are some people who hardly need any guidance but most need the leader to set out the project, their expectations, including timelines, and the reporting they will require. Good empowerment means you have to do some good work up front with the person or team you're empowering.

My experience is that many good people in Christian bodies do not want to force themselves forward, they prefer to be asked to take on a project, but if asked, and if asked by the leader, they are normally delighted. They also don't mind reporting back on their project, in fact they often see this as a kind of recognition, an acknowledgement that what they are doing is important. They see it as confirmation that the leader is interested in the project and wants to be updated and to make suggestions on the work as it goes along. Good leaders develop others by giving responsibility. Truly great leaders will have developed other leaders by giving responsibility, coaching, guiding and encouraging. When hiring, try and check out as much as you can about a leader's record and especially their record in developing others.

We have spent some time on the importance of working through others and the things that are likely to make this successful. This has been deliberate as this understanding and quality is critical for anyone who aspires to lead any organisation regardless of its size. People who value others and can communicate this are likely to bring a great deal of positive energy to your organisation.

Remember people are different

When working through others, great leaders will also remember and appreciate that people are different. They have different ways of absorbing information, behaving in meetings and have different needs and motivators. This is a complex area but the essential point is that the leader needs to get to know their people, how they operate and also needs remember that not everyone will have the same outlook and style as they do.

There is a lot of research to show that people can have a variety of different styles and preferences and how these will impact how they behave in the organisation, both in one-to-one situations and when working in wider teams. Some people are introverts and prefer to observe events and adopt a cautious, precise and disciplined approach. Some are extroverts, they want to lead, they may dislike detail, and want to drive to the objective as quickly as possible. Still others may like to be the supporter in a group, doing tasks discreetly, building relationships, being loyal and having a very team focused approach. There are also some who will want to inspire others, do tasks collaboratively and use their persuasion and creative skills.

If you have a new group it's worth doing some research to understand differing personality types and then work with your group to understand the character of your group members. This can be enormously powerful in helping to understand why people behave as they do and why they react to ideas and initiatives as they do. We have probably all been in situations where a new idea is floated and some sign up for it immediately and wonder aloud how it can be implemented, whilst others react very little at the time but come back later to test and understand the idea more. Their initial lack of response does not always indicate a rejection of the idea, but might merely be that they need time to process it.

Not only does a leader need to understand how a person is wired to work effectively with them, they also need to understand how this will make different team members behave in meetings and group working. Understanding this dynamic will really help to understand how the group can work most effectively.

On the subject of people being different there is one more factor that Christian leaders also need to bear in mind. Simply put it is this; people are at different stages on their walks of faith. Their level of Christian maturity will be different and as a consequence they will require different types of communication, and may be ready for different levels of commitment. In the Gospels, Jesus seems to set a different level of task on those who have just been called, saying to John and Andrew, 'come and…see' (John 1:39) and those who have matured in faith saying, 'if anyone would come after me, he must deny himself and take up his cross and follow me' (Mark 8:34). This additional factor needs to be considered by Christian leaders when working with their teams, especially when asking people to undertake ministry work.

The standard setter

During the course of the interviews I had a wonderful discussion with Sammy Mah, the then CEO of World Relief. He shed a lot of light on many things, one of which was the need for the leader to be a source of standards.

Sammy reminded me of the story from *Tipping Point* by Malcolm Gladwell. In this best seller, the author maps out the idea of how broken windows send messages about what is acceptable. People take their cues on standards from what they see happening around them. If they are in a neighbourhood that is run down and the windows are broken, and these windows don't get repaired, then they are unlikely to respect the place and may even to add to the damage. Similarly, in an organisation people are continually watching the management to see what standards they set. Do they care the windows are broken, do they start to fix them, do they look to improve the environment or don't they care and just ignore what's going on?

The managerial lead is likely to set the tone and standard for the whole organisation. In *Tipping Point* this idea is illustrated by looking at the turn around in crime in New York City. In the 1970's, New York was at the pinnacle of its crime problem and the authorities seemed to be faced with an insurmountable task. However, the Police Chief and Transport Commissioner decided to start turning around the crime scene by showing that they would not tolerate what was happening. They decided to focus on the small things, they figured that this would show people cared and were going to take action. That crime was not going to be allowed to run out of hand.

They started by focusing on state of the subways, cleaning up cars and stations, and started to clamp down on fare dodging. By doing this they showed that the people in charge cared about the state of things and this in turn was taken up by the public in an epidemic of *lawfulness*; the majority responded positively to the message. Moreover, by clamping down on this small issue, fare dodging, they started to arrest people who were engaged in or on their way to commit bigger crimes. This in turn created a positive spiral which was built upon, so that today you can wander around most of the city and feel pretty safe as a resident or visitor.

Good managers can help set good standards and embed these by their *example and actions*, no matter how small. Again we need to seek out people with this mentality for our own organisations.

Sammy gave me his own example of this at World Relief. When he arrived there from General Motors, he found that there were things that needed to be addressed. He surprised many by choosing, as one of the first focus areas, the time and payments system. This system was cumbersome and error prone, it required a huge amount of time to remedy the errors it created and it caused huge frustration as this involved people's working time and their rewards. On investigation he found that the system was highly manual, with the data being transferred and re-entered many times by hand. This inevitably led to a lot of work and many errors. Sammy decided to invest in a system that automated the process and removed the errors.

This seemed a strange priority and starting point to many, but for him and others it was illustrative of the fact management cared about the detail of the organisation. It also showed it was committed to getting things, no matter how small, working effectively. Powerful messages are communicated by the actions of the leadership, messages that will be watched and interpreted by those working in the organisation.

We are probably all aware that performance can be massively increased by fixing the lighting in a place of work, or repainting it, and to paying attention to the detail of performance like time-keeping. The vast majority of people in any organisation want to do a good job and sometimes they are waiting to see if the leader cares and is willing to tackle those who don't want to put in good performance. If he or she is willing to tackle these things then they are likely to generate a very positive response from the vast majority of the people.

Trained and equipped

Finally, as we have mentioned before, effective leaders will be equipped to take on the role they have been hired for. If they have to run a complex organisation they will have the *training and experience* to do this. They will also want to do it and will clearly see it as part their role. Where they are not expert they will have the self-awareness to identify this and to enlist the help of others to cover this area.

If someone is going to chair the board or council of your organisation then it clearly helps if they have the experience to do this effectively. If they are going to steer strategy and set priorities then again it's helpful if they know how to do this. If they are going to effect a turnaround then some experience of this is helpful, and if they are going to overhaul the people system, experience and awareness in this area would be a plus.

People can of course have potential and may be able to grow into roles, however if the job is a leadership one, then they will at least need to be experienced in the fundamentals of leadership to fulfil the job. They can grow their knowledge of the organisation and sector but they must know what to do as a leader in order to fulfil this kind of role.

How can I apply this?

In this section we've talked a lot about the qualities of the leader and perhaps the most important is being able to build teams and work through others. In view of this the model I offer in this chapter is concerned with repairing a dysfunctional team and comes from Patrick Lencioni's book, *The Five Dysfunctions of a Team*. In this the author outlines five reasons teams why don't work as:

An absence of trust—this is the first dysfunction and is the basis for the following four. This absence of trust stems from the team's unwillingness to be vulnerable within their group. Team members are not open with each other about mistakes and weaknesses and this makes it impossible to build the foundation for trust.

Fear of conflict—the failure to build trust means that the team has a fear of conflict. Teams that lack trust are incapable of engaging in unfiltered and passionate debates about ideas. Instead they often resort to veiled discussion and guarded comments.

Lack of commitment—a lack of healthy conflict is a problem as it ensures that there is a lack of commitment. Without having aired their opinions in the course of passionate and open debate, team members rarely, if ever, buy in and commit themselves to decisions, though they may feign agreement during meetings.

Avoidance of accountability—because of a lack of real commitment and buy-in, team members develop avoidance of accountability. Without committing to a clear plan of action, even the most focused and driven people will hesitate to call their peers on actions and behaviours that seem counterproductive to the good of the team.

Inattention to results—failure to hold one another accountable creates an atmosphere where the fifth dysfunction can thrive. Inattention to results occurs when team members put their individual needs (ego, career development, recognition) or even the needs of their sub-group above the needs of the organisation as a whole.

Teamwork deteriorates even if a single dysfunction is allowed to flourish. It's like a chain with one broken link.

Now clearly the role of the leader is to help the team overcome these dysfunctions. There are a number of ways to do this:

An absence of trust—to get over this issue teams must make themselves vulnerable to one another, and confident that their respective vulnerabilities will not be used against each other.

One way of doing this is for the team to meet and share their personal histories, their dreams and motivations. Clearly this has to go beyond stating name, rank and number. In order to make this happen, the leader should start this exercise having worked out their story in some detail. If this is open, honest and revealing, the likelihood is that those who go next will follow the pattern set. I have done this myself and seen the power of it in a group of complete strangers. By the end of the session, not only have people shared openly and established a trust with each other, the group also tends to know things about one another that would take **years** of normal interaction to be revealed. This creates a real understanding and bond amongst the group—however the tone set by the leader's own story is key, he or she must lead off in the right way.

Trust can also be built by undertaking personality and behavioural questionnaires as a team and being willing to share and discuss the results. This allows an openness about self to emerge, greater understanding to take place and possibly some changes to behaviour to be agreed.

Fear of conflict—if trust has been established, the fear of conflict is likely to reduce markedly. The leader can also help the group address this issue in a number of ways. Firstly, he or she can allow time for real debate and use open questions to find out what others think. He or she will also need to demonstrate some restraint when people engage in conflict, and allow resolution to occur naturally. This will mean resisting a desire to protect members from harm, which can lead to the premature interrupting of disagreements and preventing people from developing their own coping skills. Finally, the leader also needs to model appropriate conflict behaviour, including going for the issue and not the person.

Lack of commitment—a lack of commitment is often caused when there is ambiguity around the direction and priorities, and where discussions and decisions are revisited again and again. The leader can help by ensuring clarity around direction and priorities, setting deadlines and building a culture where it's acceptable to learn from mistakes. This latter quality allows the organisation to try a few things and to be willing to change direction if they don't work out. Debates also have to be closed off by the group, having been debated adequately, and real agreement has to be sought regarding the schedules the team has set. In short, there needs to be some hard edged agreements whilst accepting that if things change then the plan will need to be adapted.

Avoidance of accountability—the most effective way of generating accountability is peer pressure. The fear of letting down teammates tends to motivate people to improve their performance. In view of this, the leader needs to ensure that clear goals and standards are published, that there are regular progress reviews, and celebrations when goals are hit.

The leader also needs to model the accountability they want to see in the team and establish a culture whereby people in the team can question each other on the delivery of their part of the process. In turn, they will respect each other so that they start to expect high standards.

Inattention to results—one way to overcome this is for the leader to ensure that results are publicly declared. They also need to be selfless and objective in their review of results and focus on the team delivering as a whole, rather than individuals within it. The leader should also establish the idea that good results will be celebrated and that failures will be openly acknowledged and learnt from. This latter thing sometimes seems to be difficult for us in Christian organisations as we seem to think being open about failures means blaming someone for these—this need not be the case; we can generate a culture which acknowledges failures and learns from them, rather than one which goes off on a long process of allocating blame.

CHAPTER 19

Support Your Leaders

Physical conditions

Assuming we hire the right leader, the question then becomes how can we effectively support this person?

Well in the base case, we can value them and their families, seek to support them and ensure that their needs are being met and that they are not suffering through poor accommodation, inadequate funding or lack of the tools to do their job. 'The labourer is worthy of his hire,' (Luke 10:7) and on this basis we should make sure that the needs of our leaders are properly met and we should demonstrate our love and support by caring about these matters.

Giving feedback

There is another way we can be supportive and that is by being not simply acquiescent but by practising real grown up relationship with our leaders.

When we have a problem with what they are doing, we should go to them rather than discuss it with everyone else. We should seek to resolve the issue with them and we should give helpful feedback. Good leaders will seek feedback because they know that no one is perfect, so there will be issues that need to be addressed.

They will be smart enough to know that when you're not getting feedback it does not mean that people are not talking about you. In fact the likelihood is that if someone is unhappy then they will be telling others, maybe a lot of others. The other thing a good leader knows is that feedback is enormously valuable, especially feedback from those you work closely with. It enables you to understand how they feel, the impact you're having on people, what people appreciate about what you're doing and what's driving them crazy. Feedback means you can increase your self-awareness and do something about the impact you're having. If there's an issue, you then have the chance to address it. So, receiving feedback is important and so is giving it.

Clearly if we're looking to be supportive through providing feedback then there is a right (and wrong) way to give it. We need to ensure it's not all negative, to make sure the person knows what we appreciate about them and what they are doing, and to offer criticism in a constructive way. We should seek to ensure our feedback is based on helpful changes that can be made. We need to be prepared to explain why these changes would help, and if possible we need to outline why they would help the person as well as the whole organisation. It would also be helpful to offer some suggestions as to how the change might be carried out.

Let's take the example of a leader who does not work enough through the people. George tries to do everything himself, and he's certainly not great at delegating and fully involving others. He's dimly aware of this but thinks that by doing everything himself he can keep control and avoid the debate (and criticism) that may come from getting others involved. As a consequence of this, he is struggling to get everything done and is creating a bottleneck. In addition, people are becoming frustrated that they are not being involved or being asked to do anything meaningful. They have started to complain to one another and are wondering what they are doing here when they are not given any real responsibility!

Here you can feedback to the person that you've observed this and that the organisation does not expect them to do everything, and in fact people would like to help out. Given this you could suggest how the leader could try this out by commissioning a few groups to take on a few key tasks and see what effect this has. All parties can benefit from the feedback. The leader starts to learn to delegate and those around start to be trusted. You may also need to walk alongside the leader so that this is a real process, supported by real empowerment, and is not just attempted in a half-hearted way. If this is the case, the benefits will be lost, as will the value of the feedback.

A couple of other thoughts on this subject; try and ensure you always give feedback face-to-face, unless this is geographically impossible. This makes it a relational interaction, and not something that is cold and remote. It also enables you to gauge reaction, and offer more explanation if this is needed. If face-to-face is not possible then try and make the feedback a conversation via the 'phone or web-link. E-mail may well be one of the worst ways of giving feedback, it takes no account of reaction and seems to be a medium in which it is very easy to be misunderstood. Remember feedback should be about the behaviour and the reaction it's creating. It is not an evaluation of the person and their character. Try to be as factual as possible and to give examples, this takes you from opinion to fact and normally enables you to discuss issues and not character.

Bill Hybels again tells an interesting story in *Axiom, Powerful Leadership Proverbs*. In this he describes the work of Catherine Johnson who wrote a book called *Lucky in Love*. In this she sought to determine what made happily married people happy in their marriages. One fact that kept coming up time and time again as she interviewed people for her book was that at some point these couples had covenanted with each other that they would vociferously disagree but refuse to destroy each other. Bill calls this disagreeing without drawing blood. Here's a great technique for us to learn as followers; the ability to respect someone enough that we'll be honest enough to disagree with them, but will do this in such a way which shows we love and respect them as a person.

Allow leaders to lead

There is another key way we can support our leaders, that is by *allowing them to lead!* Too often in Christian bodies everyone feels that they have the right to be heard and that their view should be acted upon. If their idea is not adopted then they can see this as some kind of monumental slight. This can make life tricky for leaders and flies a little in the face of most research about good practice. This research indicates that the most effective leaders use two styles in almost equal measure when running an organisation. They *push* and they *pull*, and we have to allow them the freedom to use each of these mechanisms when appropriate. Let's explore this a little further.

There are times when leaders need to push the organisation; that is to be a little autocratic. They need to tell people what to do, to sell *their* ideas to them, and to develop new concepts and to test them out with people. This all involves very little democracy and consultation, but can be relevant to some situations. A classic example of this is when a leader takes over a failing organisation. The organisation is in 'free fall' and if this is not addressed pretty quickly then there will be nothing left to save. Given this situation the leader needs to move fast, he or she needs to get the right people in the right roles, and get the wrong people out. The leader also needs to develop a clear plan for recovery, with clear milestones, and then needs the organisation to get on with implementing this plan. This is not a time for endless consultation and debate, or a time when everyone's needs and views can be taken into account. It is a time for clear and decisive action and failing to do this will allow extreme harm to befall the organisation. It may even spell the end for that body.

This focus on pushing can be very effective in the short term, and is a useful emergency measure. It is unlikely to succeed over a longer period so the *pushing* leader also needs to be able to pull the organisation along. That is, he needs to consult, and in some cases be prepared to join in with and support others' initiatives. This pull phase can happen when people have emerged from the crisis phase and now want to play a fuller and more active role in shaping the direction of the organisation.

In both phases we need to support the leader, both when he or she is being highly directive and also when they need more rounded input and participation to carry the organisation forward. Clearly, when seeking this support, the leader needs to communicate what he or she is doing and why, and to get 'buy in' for all these approaches and phases.

In addition, in terms of allowing our leaders to lead, we also need to recognise that there are some issues which we have hired the leader to oversee and we must give him authority in these matters. For example, when we hire a new pastor we expect them to decide on and ensure the delivery of the teaching programme. Many others may have a view on this, and many of these views will be helpful and should be offered to the pastor. However, we should not see a person or group try to wrest control of this teaching away from the pastor. If his teaching is false or problematic then this must be dealt with, but power struggles should not ensue because of differences over matters of taste and style. Let the leader lead.

Row the boat, don't rock it

Finally, in an organisation where we have competent leadership, we should seek to fully participate. We are called to be rowers in the boat and not to rock it in the hope that it will tip over. This may seem obvious but it is amazing how often members of a Christian body, even leading members, will be rockers rather than rowers. They will participate little in the actual work but will have an opinion on anything and everything that goes on. Often these opinions are pitched into the debate in a destructive way, a bit like a missile being launched into a target. These opinions may also be spread far and wide, causing upset, unrest and consternation.

We're sometimes in danger of being like Statler and Waldorf in the Muppet Show. These two old men sit in their box every week shouting down criticisms of the show. One of their standard refrains is that one of them says, 'great, now we've come to the good part,' the other says, 'what's that?' and the reply is, 'the end of course!' Another of these quips is that Waldorf says, 'well you've got to give them credit,' and Statler replies, 'why's that?', 'well, they're gonna keep on doing it until they get it right!'

Let's try not to be Statlers and Waldorfs! Instead, let's try to lend a hand not only in terms of giving advice but in terms of actually picking up those tasks which need volunteers. Be the person who organises the weekend away, or helps with the youth work, or gives some time to the administration of the organisation, or helps re-paint the buildings or does the washing-up—or whatever is needed.

In exchange

We should support our leaders. In exchange for this support it is hoped that leaders will recognise their need to consult and involve the members of their organisation. In addition, it is also to be hoped that they will understand and accept the need to be held accountable. Indeed good leaders need to ensure that there are real mechanisms in place to ensure accountability. They also need to ensure that they properly answer for their leadership and management of the organisation.

How can I apply this?

So, given all of this, how do we effectively support our leaders, how do we vociferously disagree without drawing blood? Well we're given a clue as to how to do this in Susan Scott's book *Fierce Conversations*—fierce in this context means real and meaningful rather than aggressive and hostile. Scott puts forward the idea that good relationships are built up one conversation at a time, each conversation we have is of value in building the relationship.

Scott is a well know consultant with an impressive track record of working with CEOs and helping to turn around businesses. Much of this she does by understanding what human interaction is going on in a business and where this is going wrong. She's then happy and to call out this behaviour to enable it to change for the better. She explains in her book that her experience has led her to see that conversations not only help build up relationships but they are really the heart of the relationship that we enjoy with others. She says, 'conversation is the relationship'. If this conversation stops, the relationship cannot grow and flourish.

Conversations only build real relationships if they are real—robust, sometimes intense, strong, passionate, and unbridled. There's a saying amongst recruiters that sometimes you see people who claim to have twenty years experience in a particular field. When you come to interview them you soon understand that in fact they have had one year's experience twenty times. That is they have kept on going round the same loop, happy to repeat what they know and not really learning anything new. Without real conversations, the same applies to relationships. How many people do you know who have polite relationships, they exchange pleasantries, chat in a friendly way, share some generalities together and after they have 'known' each other for ten years their relationship is still entirely superficial?

In her book Scott suggests seven principles for having a fierce or real conversation. I would suggest that you can take these and think through how you might apply them when dealing with your leader or leadership. Maybe you can use these principles to have real conversations with your leader and build a real relationship that will best serve them, you and the organisation.

Principle 1: Master the courage to interrogate reality

No situation or plan survives unless you're willing to take account of reality. Reality shifts all the time, people and circumstances change, and we change. We have to be willing to confront this reality and accept that it will change and influence our plans. Life is not straightforward, it takes twist and turns and we have to be willing to accept this and adapt to it rather than just clinging on to what we want the world to be like. Doggedly hanging on to what we want means we will not engage with reality and we will also make it difficult to engage with others because we'll want the world to work our way no matter what happens.

Principle 2: Come out from behind yourself in the conversation and make it real

This is a rather long way of saying that we need to be real in conversations. We need to be honest and open and share of ourselves. Unreal conversations will not advance the relationship and will not enable real change to occur.

Principle 3: Be here; be prepared to be nowhere else

When you speak to someone try speaking and listening as if this is the most important conversation of your life. If you participate as if it matters. it will matter and the outcome is going to be a lot stronger. So focus on what's happening and don't drift off thinking of something else. If you don't have time for the conversation at that time, say so and schedule it for a time when you can pay attention. In conversations what is said is only a small part of what's going on—body language, signals, mood are as important.

Principle 4: Tackle your toughest challenge today

Burnout does not occur because we're solving problems, it occurs because we're trying to solve the same problem over and over again. The problem named is the problem solved. Identify and then confront real obstacles in your path. When you're doing this, value the people you're working with and try to avoid having 'an axe to grind.' Focus on the problem and solving it, not on your preconceived agenda.

Principle 5: Obey your instincts

Your instincts are sending you messages all the time, pay attention to these and share these thoughts with others. Your instincts are like a radar screen showing up images that may well become real.

Principle 6: Take responsibility for your emotional wake

Sometimes you don't remember saying something that might have had a devastating impact on someone who came to you for advice and guidance. These conversations set the relationship. Learn to deliver messages with clarity, conviction, and compassion, avoid attaching an emotional load to it.

Principle 7: Let silence do the heavy lifting

When there's a whole lot of talking going on, conversations can be very empty. Memorable conversations need breathing space. Slow down the conversation and allow insights to occur between the words and you can really understand what the conversation needs to be about.

CHAPTER 20

Use Good Tools

As we have discussed, Christian organisations often lack good systems and processes because they are not understood, not valued, or are actively resisted. This can create serious issues that can be addressed without building an unhelpful and stifling bureaucracy. Professional systems and process can be helpful. We need to be selective in choosing these processes and need to ensure that they don't become an end in themselves. Having said this, there are many tools out there which others have developed and which can help us build effective organisations.

Let's just consider a few things that it would be helpful to have in place.

Professional recruitment

Generally, Christian organisations do not have thousands or even hundreds of staff. Significant organisations may have less than a hundred paid people. Given this, every staff member really does count, and hiring the right people is crucial.

During the interviews all interviewees referred to the importance of getting the right people into Christian organisations. They spoke of the power that was released when this was achieved. Having said this, in many Christian organisations the hiring process is often sub-optimal for a number of reasons. Sometimes, people have not put any process in place. They operate on a 'gut feel' basis and think that this is a good modus operandi. People also feel God will deliver the right person without us using our best human endeavours. Whilst we should clearly pray, and seek God's guidance when looking to fill any role, we should also use the abilities He has given us to undertake this process as professionally as we can.

A good recruitment process normally starts with a *job description* that explains what the role is. It also will speak to the technical skills and personal qualities being sought in the job holder. Sometimes Christian hiring is carried out without this document or the document lacks real clarity and focus. Normally it's better to have a few key accountabilities in this description rather than just throw in the twenty-eight tasks you think you want covered. The problem with a *shopping list* is that it's hard to see what's important.

The benefits of a good job description are many fold, you get clarity as to the person you are seeking. The recruitment group has a chance to develop a common view, and to work to this. The candidate knows what you want and also, importantly, what you don't want. In addition, you have a yardstick to help design the recruitment process, and if you're seeking x, y and z in a person then you need to know this and also how you're going to test for it. It also gives you the basis of developing *role clarity* for the person once they take up the role. Assume you want to hire a youth worker to run Christian clubs in local schools. This person is going to have a different brief and profile to a youth worker working with your own in-house groups. They will need to be more able to reach the un-churched, they will need to be skilled in dealing with the school authorities and will need to be able to operate with different kinds of materials.

Once the job description is fixed then spend time on the recruitment process. Agree who will be involved, who will ask what, will there be testing, how will you acquire actual evidence that a person has the experience and character you want. Simple interviewing is generally not a great measure of a person, especially if the interviews are fairly short. The more time you talk with a person, the more views you get, the more you ask about specifics, and for examples, the addition of testing and profiling all help get to a better decision. This may sound a little time consuming or 'over-professional' and you need to get the balance of this right. However, think about hiring a pastor who might be with you 10, 15 or even 20 years. How much time and effort is it worth investing in getting this hire right?

Try also to make the process two-way; the person also needs to decide if they want to join you. Encourage questions, let them get multiple views of the place and the job, ensure their families are on board with the decision. Many roles fail not because the terms and conditions are wrong but because the spouse is not happy.

It is also worth doing your *homework,* and undertaking proper reference checks, and find out what the person has done before. Have they really climbed Mount Everest, and negotiated a settlement to the Middle-east crisis or was this a bit of hyperbole? More seriously, is there something around their past practice which you need to know to protect your community going forward?

Getting references can be tough in the modern world where referees are so concerned about litigation that they may make only the blandest statements on paper. My practical advice is to seek verbal references as well as written ones, and to seek them from different sources. This latter point is to help ensure a full picture but also to be fair to the candidate. You may talk to one person who has a crossed wire with them and a particular viewpoint that is not universally shared or agreed with. If you do uncover something that is significant then you need to try and validate this. Take account of what you hear rather than just discounting it. If there is a problem, in all conscience, people will generally feel the need to highlight this.

Jill Garfitt was kind enough to look at my draft text and pointed out the biblical underpinning of these good recruitment techniques. In Acts 1:21-26 we see that the disciples need to replace Judas, the betrayer of Jesus, in the leadership. Peter quotes from Psalms and then there is a process. They set the criteria, 'choose one of the men who have been with us the whole time.' They prayed for guidance, 'show us which one you have chosen,' and finally, 'they cast lots.' This casting of lots was a seeking guidance—not unlike having clear criteria and searching interview questions. This does not mean that we don't seek God's will through prayer, but does mean that we see guidance and confirmation by using the tools we have available to us.

Similarly, in Acts 6:1-6 we see the disciples setting up clear criteria for seven who would be called to administer the church. Their role is made clear, both what it is and what it is not; *the disciples will be the ones who focus on 'prayer and ministry of the word.'* The process for selecting these people is also made clear, as is the personal qualities that they have to have demonstrated. It is also clear who will choose them and who will be responsible for commissioning them. This is no unstructured and arbitrary process.

Performance Management

Performance management (appraisals, personal reviews) or rather the lack of it was a huge subject for many of my interviewees.

They cited this as one of the fundamental causes of people problems in Christian organisations. They saw that this lack of performance management meant many issues went unaddressed, as there was no mechanism for holding a person accountable and no expectation that they would need to answer for their behaviour and performance. Moreover, a lack of performance management meant that objectives were often not clear, role clarity was lost and a meaningful dialogue on how the individual was doing did not take place.

For anyone who has been in business for a number of years, a lack of this most fundamental process is surprising. To understand it we need to understand the culture of many Christian organisations, which hold that this kind of process would run counter to trusting people and would be hard to do given the nature of their work. It may also be felt that it is not clear who should undertake the review. This kind of thinking seems pretty weak and may be indicative of a more fundamental issue. Many in Christian organisations don't like confrontation and see this kind of review as leading to inevitable confrontation with the person being appraised.

This does seem to be pretty wrong-headed thinking, and may also spring from a lack of experience in this area. Many organisations are very hesitant and fearful when they first introduce performance management. They think it will mean bosses are given too much power, people will be too harshly judged and so on. Clearly performance management in itself in not the solution to all ills, it has to be done well. But if it is done well then it can have great benefits.

In terms of mechanics, to do this well I suggest that it needs to give an opportunity, ideally up front, for the individual to say how they feel. What do they think has gone well, what has gone less well, what do they think should be their objectives in the coming year, and what training development and support would they like. For Christian organisations it is probably also helpful to find out how they feel about their ministry and how they are being supported. It's feedback for the boss as well as an opportunity for the individual to flag where they are.

Ideally there will also be a mechanism for gaining feedback about the individual from multiple sources. That is, the individual will nominate others who can comment on their performance and have these comments fed into the process. If you engage in this kind of 360-degree feedback you need to decide if it's given anonymously or not. My view is that it is normally more meaningful if it's anonymous. In these circumstances, feedback tends to be more open and helpful. I have been in a situation where we used both mechanisms for 360-feedback. When the feedback was identified and credited to people then the Christian desire to say nice things kicked in and what was offered was often of little value as it tended to be very anodyne. Ironically, by seeking to say nice things and be nice, people did not help the person to address issues and move their development forward. I don't believe feedback should be destructive but if there are things that need to be worked on then these do need to be flagged.

Once the individual and appraiser have the person's own input then they can meet. The appraiser needs to prepare for this discussion and bring performance issues, objectives, development and support needs to the table. During the meeting the appraiser and individual need to talk and work to agree all of these issues so that they can record an agreed document for the future.

This is the mechanistic part of performance management. In terms of the attitudinal part, the appraiser has to be prepared to make this a real event.

It cannot just be a meeting where the individual is told they are marvellous, but a meeting where strengths are highlighted, objectives agreed and where issues are tackled and corrective actions agreed upon. This attitude and spirit should also be shared by the individual, who will also hopefully see this as an opportunity to have their voice heard and their issues acted upon. This performance review process should not be a one-way street, it should be a two-way, grown up dialogue that takes both parties to a better place. A good process and open discussion will hopefully ensure that everyone is clear about what needs to be done next. If done really well this can form a real platform not only for good practice but also for healthy relationships. Good performers don't just want to be told everything is great, they want specifics and to agree how they can be stretched and grow in the future. They also want to know what they need to work on.

Performance management should not be limited to one formal review a year. Ideally it should be an on-going dialogue between the boss and their report. To get good at this you need to work on it, it's not an easy thing to do and it takes practice. This should not discourage people from starting and developing this tool and the dialogue it brings. Used well it will help start to change that central problem which we seem to face in Christian bodies. That is an inability or unwillingness to address difficult issues, especially issues of performance and behaviour.

Confronting these issues is healthy and you may be pleasantly surprised that sometimes people are doing the wrong thing not through any ill intent but because they have not had feedback and were not aware there was a problem. Sometimes, of course, they will be fully aware that they are off track, in which case you still need to tackle it!

Investing in people

Any great organisation will have process for developing and investing in its people. Processes for understanding what capabilities the organisation needs and how it will grow them, processes for understanding the individual's developmental needs and how these will be met. It will continually be developing people to ensure they are fully equipped in their current role, equipped to meet their next role, and take on challenges that will arise.

Many Christian bodies have limited time and resources and therefore feel they cannot afford to train their people. This is likely to be a false economy as people are not being refreshed and developed. Instead of growing and gaining 10, 15 or 20 years' experience, they may end up just repeating the same year's experience many times. Much training can be done on the job, indeed some of the most relevant development happens this way as it is immediate and is practised. There are also many cost effective ways to train your people; mentoring, coaching, using the expertise which you have in the organisation, taking advantage of very cost effective programmes provided by bodies which are focused on the not-for profit sector and who therefore keep their costs down.

The web gives us a great opportunity to take on board web-based training. There are now many great materials out there like Harvard Lingos; materials that are provided to commercial organisations and which are also provided to the not-for-profit sector at a much reduced price. So price and opportunity is a lot easier than it was in the past.

The point here is to ensure that this issue is addressed and that a system is in place to grow and develop the most valuable, and probably expensive, resource you have; your people.

How can I apply this?

Perhaps the greatest challenge for organisations struggling to move their relationships beyond niceness is to have an effective performance review system. The very thought of this is often enough to throw people into an apoplexy, but rest assured it need not be so. Such a tool should not only help you to give feedback to a staff member, but should also help you to understand where they are emotionally and in their thinking. Clearly, in performance reviews the tool you use is less important than the quality of discussion that takes place. Nevertheless, a good tool and a commitment to the process can really help ensure the review is beneficial to all parties.

Getting good at performance reviews is an iterative process so don't expect that your first go at this will be perfect, both you (as appraiser) and the individual will probably find that you get better at this process each time you do it. Key to the conversation is that both parties come to this looking to value the other and being prepared to celebrate what is positive as well as to be honest about where development is needed and improvement required.

I have included below a summary of the main elements of the performance review system that I was asked to design for use in our own church. One thing which was modified from the first draft is that the clergy asked for more input into the process via their own self-evaluation form and we built this in. Having done this, the self-appraisal has proved to be invaluable in understanding where an individual is in their own thinking, where they are emotionally and how supported they feel.

The process consists of 4 documents:

1. Guidelines on how to carry out the review
2. Self-appraisal form
3. Feedback form
4. An objectives and development form

Here is a distillation of each document, and readers should feel very free to take these elements and adapt them to their own needs.

The guidelines:

- Overview of the process
- Description of the forms involved and their purpose
- Description of who should do what
- Guidelines for handling the documents i.e. drafts and feedback forms to be destroyed and final copies to be held by staff member, appraiser, and if appropriate by the appraiser's boss

The self-appraisal form—an opportunity for the staff member to record prior to the appraisal meeting:

- Their major achievements and accomplishments for the year
- Their missed opportunities for the year
- Their perceived key strengths in the role
- Their perceived development needs
- What they would want their objectives to be in the coming year
- In what way they felt well supported by the church leadership over the past year
- In what way they would have welcomed more/better support from the church leadership in the past year
- How they currently feel about their role and the support being given

Completed by the staff member and a copy handed to appraiser before the appraisal meeting to allow him/her to see the staff member's view of things

The feedback form—a feedback completed by 4 to 6 church family members, nominated by the staff member. These people asked to feedback to the <u>appraiser</u> on this form—their feedback is then amalgamated and made anonymous. The staff member should receive amalgamated feedback, not individual inputs:

- Feedback on what they see as the staff member's strengths
- Feedback on what they see as his/her development needs

An objectives and development form—competed by the appraiser but must be agreed and signed by the staff member. This form completed after the appraisal discussion has taken place, covering:

- Staff member's strengths
- Staff member's development needs, and how these will be met
- Evaluation of previous year's performance against objectives
- Objectives for the coming year—SMART i.e. specific, measurable, agreed, realistic, and time defined

CHAPTER 21

Grown up Volunteering

THE ENGAGEMENT AND use of volunteers can be highly beneficial to an organisation. It can provide a pool of motivated and talented people who give themselves to helping the organisation fulfil its goals and mission, and do so with an extraordinary degree of dedication.

Valuing organisation

However, as we have already seen, leading volunteers is not easy and has some unique challenges. Perhaps the first thing to overcome when leading volunteers is that many in voluntary organisations are not too keen on the concept of organisation. They see organisation as being synonymous with management, and they see this as being authoritarian, smacking of business and bureaucracy. They prefer to emphasise the idea of voluntary above organisation, that is they see the ends are important and not the means, i.e. the systems and structures that deliver them. Indeed many volunteers will be convinced that they don't need managing and don't need an organisation, they serve a cause and they should be able to do this in any way they see fit. In Christian organisations people can also see the organisation as a family, and they rationalise that families don't need management or organisation—they just find their own way forward, or they do if they are blessed. Charles Handy's excellent book *Understanding Voluntary Organisations* speaks in a clear way about how volunteers can perceive their organisation and about how they can be effectively engaged.

The first challenge you may face in engaging volunteers is in establishing the legitimacy of having any kind of organisation and structure. The way to tackle this seems to be to frame the organisation in terms that people can relate to. Rather than presenting it in business terms as a machine that has plans, controls and uses people as resources to achieve its end, present it as what it really is, or should be. That is a living community with a common purpose, a community made up of members with their own minds and needs. Emphasise the idea of a uniting culture, shared values and goals, networks and working together for a common vision. Remember volunteers are planets around a sun—you have to communicate with them, involve them, motivate them, show them that by doing things together we can be more effective and also get them to sign up to fulfilling a mission which all believe in and want to see carried out. In terms of Christian organisations, our common faith and desire to live this out should give us the strongest of starting points.

The contract

With volunteers we also need to be aware of the psychological contract. Put simply, people have expectations of themselves and the organisation. They expect to see a balance between the energy they put into their work and the way the organisation meets their expectations. In this model people are willing to give a lot if their expectations are being met. However if people just work hard and do not have their expectations met, then burn out and disillusionment tends to follow. With volunteers, their expectations are not financial rewards; rather they are the motivating factors identified by many researchers. If we take just one of these, Herzberg, then we can see that these motivational factors include; recognition, self-fulfilment, the opportunity for creativity, achievement, involvement and influence. If you're motivating and leading volunteers you need to keep these needs front of mind and seek to have them fulfilled. In this way you can benefit from the positive energy generated by this group.

When you pay staff you have what Charles Handy calls a *calculative* contract with them i.e. they are there because they are paid to be there. Of course they will have other motivations for working for you but this basic deal is at the core of what's happening. In terms of volunteers, the contract is *co-operative*. They are there because they agree with the goals of the organisation, and the people who work there. In this latter case it is harder to tell people what to do, indeed this co-operative deal means that these people have to be managed and led in a different way. Here are some things that might help when leading and coaching volunteers:

Empowerment—good volunteers are unlikely to mind having a clarity about their mission and what's expected of them. They will want freedom to define how they achieve the task they have taken on but will and should expect interest and *parameters* from the leadership. This does not have to be a 'straight-jacket', indeed it can be liberating. If I understand the framework in which I'm operating and what I'm expected to deliver then I actually have a lot of freedom about how I carry out the mission I have been given. It will be important to spend time *agreeing* with volunteers what they will do and how they will operate. As part of this you need to listen to them about how they want to do things. Indeed, you may want to show flexibility with regard to their approach. This could be motivational for them and could release innovation and new ideas. Things are likely to go well if you are clear as to what you're doing at the outset and how it will work—agreeing the rules up front is important for both the leader and the volunteer and provides a great reference point as the project progresses.

Goals—people like targets, without something to aim for then work is just a job. These targets or goals should be ones people have accepted and own. One effective way of achieving this is to let people set their own targets, or have a significant hand in this process. If you have done a lot of personal reviews you will know that people tend to set themselves tougher targets than their leaders would. The targets should be relatively short term so that they remain meaningful and live. Once the targets are set, check in with people about how they are going. Don't make this every five minutes so it seems like micro-management but do set time aside to spend with the volunteer or voluntary team to see what progress is being made.

This is not only good for keeping the project on track, it is also a kind of recognition. Good volunteers will want to know that you care about their project, that you are interested enough to check in, that what they are doing is important enough to get the attention of the leadership. This checking in should be done in a meaningful way, which I think means being prepared to offer support but also *constructive* challenge, in terms of thoughts and ideas to help the project along.

Finally, we also need to spend time making sure that the volunteers understand the vision of the organisation and how their goals fit with this and will help to deliver it. Given that the relationship with volunteers is less transactional than with paid staff, we need to ensure that they are on board with what we're trying to achieve and aligned with our direction and purpose.

Feedback—give genuine praise, try to do this very soon after the event and make it as specific as possible. If praise is specific (i.e. it talks to an actual action or event) people will tend to value it far more than the general statement that everyone is doing very well. Use a lot more praise than criticism, praise is good for the ego and self-esteem and this in turn is good for working relationships and effectiveness. Praise also transmits respect and, as we've said, we can't legislate for what we get, rather only for what we give; give the best you can. This does not mean you cannot and should not give negative feedback if it is necessary, but remember; direct this at the action or the issue and not at the person. Indeed, work hard to make sure they know you value them even though you weren't happy with a particular incident.

Take account of differences—people are different and they want different things out of their life and work. In view of this, don't assume that everyone is you and has your wants and needs. Take time to find out what makes people tick and try to ensure that you fulfil the psychological contract by helping them to meet their needs. In this way you're also likely to generate a lot of positive energy for the organisation and its cause.

Use skills wisely

Volunteers bring many skills that they have acquired in many places; work, home, through friendships, and through life experience. We should aim to use these skills wisely and work with a person to determine where they can best serve.

Let's take an example. Sally is an experienced marketing manager and knows a lot about effective internal and external communications. When she joins the church, people realise that she has something to offer. However, no real analysis is done regarding her skills and she's asked to help out with the children's work. She accepts this, even though it does not really speak to her, because she knows the work is important, there is a need in that area and she wants to help out. She does OK, but the irony is that the church has a real need to improve its internal and external communications. Sally could easily fulfil this role, and make a significant positive impact. However, as this has not been properly explored with her then this opportunity is lost.

Obviously, it may be that sometimes people want to serve in areas where they are not experts and they may also want a humble task. The senior manager may not want to play this role in church, they may well be happy to direct the traffic in the car park. They may well they want to serve in this way, but often a mismatch occurs because we have a need to fill and don't work out what a person can do and how they best can serve. This can mean that the person's motivation falls away and we lose their contribution. We need to fit the right volunteer to the right role wherever possible. In this way they will be motivated and we will get their best contribution. We will also, hopefully, be matching skills to needs.

Let's not expect someone to run and own our planning process if they have no experience of this. Even if they step forward and want to take this on, we must ensure, for their own good and ours, that the task is not one they are going to fail at. This seems simple to say but there's a lot of evidence around us of people being asked to do things that they are not suited to or equipped for.

So volunteerism is a powerful gift, but you have to devote time up front to making sure everyone knows what their role is, what they have to deliver, how they are accountable and how the communication process will work.

How can I apply this?

As you can see, my key contention is that in managing volunteers the psychological contract needs to be clear, agreed, and fulfilled by both parties.

Below is a letter created by a group of volunteer organisers to try and express what they think a volunteer wants to know when signing up to a new project—i.e. the basis of the psychological contract. This work is from *Involve, February 1985*, and you might want to ask yourself how many of these questions you answer when engaging a volunteer to undertake a task or project!

Dear Organisation,

When I begin volunteering, please outline the following:

- What will I have to do?
- How much time will I have to give?
- What do I do if something goes wrong?
- What training are you going to give me?
- After I have been volunteering for a while, will you encourage me to take the initiative in suggesting new ways of doing things?
- How will you build up and maintain my confidence?
- Will you help me to evaluate my skills?
- Is there a support group for volunteers?
- Will you let me know my limitations when it's time to ask for help?
- Have you thought of advertising our services/skills more widely?
- If I am given responsibility within the organisation, how will you support me?
- If I get tired of what I'm doing, will you help me to leave gracefully or give me a new challenge?

Yours voluntarily…

I don't think you have to be able to answer every question with every volunteer—e.g. some people may come equipped for the role and require little or no training. However the list is useful in showing that establishing the psychological contract with volunteers and managing them takes time and commitment from the leader. You don't have to undertake the project or task yourself—there would then be little point in seeking out a volunteer! However, time does need to be dedicated to setting out and agreeing the task in hand, to monitoring progress and to offering emotional support and encouragement.

This clearly requires an investment of time on the part of the leader. However, provided the right volunteer with the right skills has been selected, this is an investment which is likely to deliver a huge return in terms of achieving the task, generating enthusiasm, and building great relationships. Therefore it looks like an investment worth making!

CHAPTER 22

Negotiation

WHEN MANAGING PEOPLE there will be times when we need to negotiate a settlement with others. We will clearly not always come to all issues with the same views, opinions, and passions. We may well find that there are two different sides of an argument, with two very different viewpoints. In these circumstances we need to negotiate and consult.

William Ury, in his book *Getting Past No*, offers some helpful ideas on this, especially in the chapter entitled 'Build them a Golden Bridge.' Here, Ury talks of the obstacles to reaching an agreement and he describes them as follows:

Not his idea—the idea under debate was not generated by the other party and may simply be rejected because 'it was not invented here.'

Unmet interests—you overlook the other party's basic interests.

Fear of losing—the other party does not want to be made to look bad, especially in front of their supporters.

Too much too fast—your counterpart may resist because the decision seems too big and the time too short. They may feel that it is just easier to say no.

In this situation you need to build a bridge that spans the gap between you, one that your counterpart can cross. You then need to persuade them to make this journey. Let's take a look at some of the keys to this bridge building:

Involve your opponent

One thing that can be the kiss of death for negotiation is a failure to involve the other side in finding the solution. Normally it is very detrimental to announce a solution to an issue without consulting and inviting the ideas of the other party. This is likely to generate outright rejection, regardless of the brilliance of the solution.

Far better is to ask for the other party's ideas and to build on these. Resist the temptation to tell the other person what they should be doing. I did this once when I was frustrated at how a group were handling an issue. I thought they were not sticking to what had been agreed and were making something that should be straightforward too complicated. I decided to take the chairperson aside and tell her what I felt the group should be doing. Immediately I did this, I could feel this would not work; they wanted to be the authors of their own solution and I could feel any personal authority I had draining away.

Ury says 'negotiation is more about asking than telling.' The simplest way to involve the other party is to ask them what they would do, what they see as the solution, how they would reconcile both sides' interests. This draws them into being problem solvers. Try then to build on these solutions, taking the ones which are most effective and generating agreement around these. This does not mean short changing your own ideas, rather it means finding a way through which will be acceptable to all sides.

You can add to this process by asking for constructive criticism and offering some choices to the other party. Even if these choices are of a minor nature, for example where and when to meet, they create an atmosphere of co-operation and consultation. This will prove crucial when you come to the main points of the agreement.

Satisfy unmet interests

Try not to overlook any unmet interests; they are likely to de-rail any agreement in the end. Also, don't assume that you will immediately understand what these interests are.

A typical example of this shared with me can be seen when handling a member of staff leaving. Usually, it would be assumed that his concern would focus on his own leaving and what he would do next. This was, of course, partly true but he was more concerned about the team he left behind and how they would be led once he was gone. He was actually ready to move on to a new challenge in a new location but did not want to let down those left behind. Once this was realised and effort was put into demonstrating how his role would be filled, and funded, then progress started to be made on the move. He was also reassured that the group he left behind would continue to be supported in their mission.

When we have conflicting views, our opponents can seem very frustrating and irrational. They seem completely self-centred, and unwilling to be reasonable! Try and avoid falling into this trap—it's unlikely to lead to a successful outcome. Rather, try and see things from the point of view of your opponent and understand what will motivate them.

Motivations may take many forms, and many times they are founded on very basic human needs. This might be recognition, being properly consulted and involved. Remember we talked earlier about how people will sometimes (I think often) adopt a course of action which is different to the one they originally wanted if they feel they have been consulted, and if they feel someone has taken the trouble to sit down and explain the new plan and the reasons in its favour.

Saving face

People often need to save face if they have been involved in a negotiation, especially if they are representing others. Joe Gormley, a British trade unionist, used to have a great phrase; 'always ensure your opponent has their bus fare home.' By this he meant don't take everything in the negotiation, even if you feel you can. Always leave something for your opponent, some thing that will help them to accept the agreement. Try and think ahead to how you can help your opponent position their acceptance of a deal as a victory.

William Ury outlines several face-saving devices in his book. Explain, on your opponent's behalf, how circumstances have changed and therefore how they have been reasonable to change their own stance to accommodate this. Ask for third party recommendations from a mediator. This neutral person can apply a solution that both parties can accept, as there is no loss of face if they have agreed to mediation and to abide by its outcome. Use a standard of fairness that is acceptable to all parties. This may mean both sides need to compromise, but is also likely to allow both parties to save face.

Go slow to go fast

If a lot needs to be decided in a short time, then break the process into a series of short steps. This allows a little to be digested at a time. Gradually these small parts are digested one at a time, and before long, real progress has been made. In addition to this, don't ask for a final commitment on changes until the end and, at the end, don't rush the negotiation. Allow people time to adapt and come along with you, don't rush them and either get them off balance or make them feel that they are being 'rail-roaded.' If you do this the shutters are likely to go up and you will end up with a resounding 'no!'

In addition to Ury's advice, I would add a couple of other thoughts:

How to win an argument

Mary Buffet and David Clark, in their book *Warren Buffet's Management Secrets*, talk about how this very wealthy and powerful man learnt early on that the best way to win an argument was not to have one in the first place! Self-evident you might think, but what they meant by this was that rather than start by taking issue with someone, it is better to agree with them first off. By doing this you establish common ground and by listening to them you will often get them to listen to your point of view.

If you can listen to a person and respect their opinions, even if you don't agree with these opinions, you're likely to get them to relax and to hear your position. In the book, the authors say that the American Founding Father Benjamin Franklin, who sought to engage in conversations rather than arguments, has influenced Warren Buffet in this approach.

If your objective is to have your point of view heard and acted upon, then an argument is normally a very ineffective tool, as often when we argue, listening goes out of the window and people's positions harden. If the same topic is approached as a conversation, especially a conversation where you ensure the other person is listened to and their ideas acknowledged, then it's likely that listening will take place, that there will be give and take and that an agreement will be reached. I am sure that, like me, you've seen people arguing ferociously when it appears that they very nearly agree with each other—they just can't see this because they have become so emotionally wrapped up in the argument!

Let the other party know you value them

There are many ways that we can *genuinely* communicate to another party that we value them even if we disagree with their current idea. Ideally, if you have dealt with a person for a long time, you will have good emotional capital with them. They will know that you value them and the friendship that exists between you. This will allow for the most robust of exchanges and disagreements to take place without the trust between you being broken.

A friend of mine once had an audacious plan that our church could save a local primary school from closure. This required a huge commitment of time, money and credibility. He wanted my support in the church council for the project but I had a lot of misgivings. The project looked like it could be a huge distraction for the church, it would absorb a lot of time and energy and we had other projects to worry about. I wondered if we had the expertise to take on this project. The previous owners of the school were experts in the education field and had not made the school work. We were not experts and it was not clear to me what we could add and if we would know what we were doing. In addition, there was the financial challenge involved in taking on the debts of the school.

However, we have a strong friendship and had been through many challenges together. Because of this, I was open to his ideas and arguments, he worked hard to answer all the challenges put to him and in the end I supported the project both in the church council and as a member of the school board.

Sometimes, we do not have a long history with another person and so cannot rely on emotional capital. In these circumstances, we have to show we value the other person by listening to them and their ideas. By ensuring we understand their arguments and input, we are genuinely seeking to work with them to find a solution to our differences. They need to feel that, whatever the outcome, this is about the issue in hand and not about how we value them; whatever our disagreements about the issues, we value them for who they are.

How can I apply this?

We have talked about negotiating in this chapter and one further thing that might be helpful to readers is to take a look at their own negotiating style. This kind of self-awareness will enable you to understand better where you come from and to modify your approach accordingly if this is necessary. I have enclosed below a self-assessment aid to help you look at your own negotiation style—I am grateful to Kate Marshal and the MaST organisation for this model.

SELF ASSESSMENT OF KEY NEGOTIATION ATTITUDES

In each element put 1 against the statement, which you consider to be most like you;

2 against the statement next most like you and so on up to 5 which is least like you,

(i.e. score 1—5 in each of the 6 elements).

Element 1: Decisions

A   I accept decisions of others.
B   I place high value on maintaining good relations.
C   I place high value on making decisions that stick.
D   I search for workable, even though not perfect, decisions.
E   I place high value on getting sound creative decisions that result in understanding and agreement.

Element 2: Convictions

A   I listen for and seek out ideas, opinions and attitudes different from my own, I have clear convictions but respond to sound ideas by changing my mind.
B   I go along with opinions, attitudes and ideas of others or avoid taking sides.
C   I prefer to accept opinions, attitudes and ideas of others rather than push my own.
D   I stand up for my ideas, opinions, attitudes, even though it sometimes results in stepping on toes.
E   When ideas, opinions or attitudes different from my own appear, I initiate middle ground positions.

Element 3: Conflict

A   When conflict arises, I try to identify reasons for it and to resolve underlying causes.
B   When conflict arises, I try to be fair but firm and to get an equitable solution.
C   When conflict arises, I try to cut it off to win my position.
D   I try to avoid generating conflict, but when it does appear, I try to soothe feelings and to keep people together.

E   When conflict arises, I try to remain neutral or stay out of it.

Element 4: Emotions (temper)

A   When things are not going right, I defend, resist or come back with counter arguments.
B   Under tension, I feel unsure which way to turn or shift to avoid further pressure.
C   Because of the disturbance tensions can produce, I react in a warm and friendly way.
D   When annoyed, I contain myself, though my impatience is visible.
E   By remaining neutral, I rarely get stirred up.

Element 5: Humour

A   My humour aims at maintaining friendly relations or, when strains do arise, it shifts attention away from the serious side.
B   My humour is seen by others as rather pointless.
C   My humour fits the situation and gives perspective, I retain a sense of humour even under pressure.
D   My humour sells myself or a position.
E   My humour is hard hitting.

Element 6: Effort

A   I rarely lead but extend help.
B   I drive myself and others.
C   I put out enough effort to get by.
D   I seek to maintain a good steady pace.
E   I exert vigorous effort and others join in.

NEGOTIATION GRID
Summary of Personal Ratings

Transfer the ratings you have given to element 1, Decisions, along the grid. Enter your rating for A in the first box then enter each rating along the Decision line. Next move onto element 2 matching your rating to the relevant A, B, C, D, E, box. Complete the grid, then total the columns which should add across to 90.

ELEMENT	1/1	1/9	5/5	9/1	9/9
1. Decisions	A	B	D	C	E
2. Convictions	B	C	E	D	A
3. Conflict	E	D	B	C	A
4. Emotions	E	C	B	A	D
5. Humour	B	A	D	E	C
6. Effort	C	A	D	B	E
Total					

Your lowest score indicates your prime Negotiating Style your next lowest score indicates your secondary style.

NEGOTIATING STYLES

The discussion and analysis of Negotiating Styles is based upon the method of measurement put forward by Blake and Mouton in their book *The Managerial Grid*.

The grid is defined like this

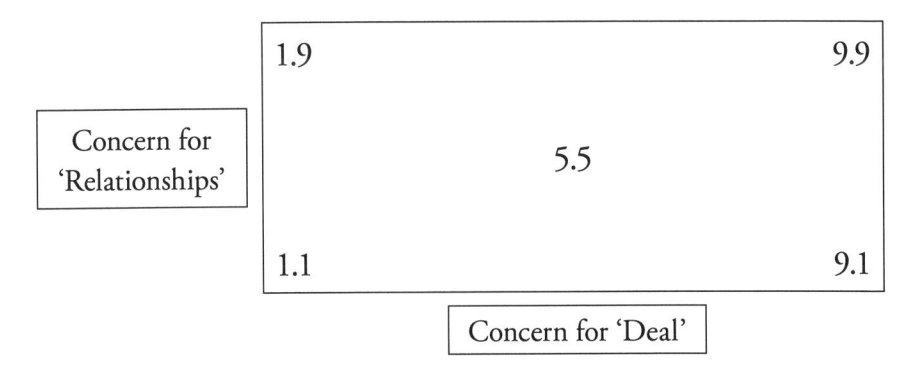

Concern for 'Relationships'	1.9	9.9
	5.5	
	1.1	9.1

Concern for 'Deal'

Five locations on the grid are taken to provide illustrations of the variations in Management Style.

1.9 Maximum concern for "Relationships"—minimum for "Deal". This is based on the assumption that if you are 'nice' to people they will give you a better deal. Lose/Win.

1.1 No interest in "Relationships" or achieving a negotiated "Deal"— Take it or leave it attitude! Lose/Lose

9.1 Maximum concern for "Deal" and minimum for "Relationship". Achieve the best position possible at the expense of possible future negotiations. Win/Lose.

5.5 The key word here is "Compromise". An attempt is made to get some sort of workable mix between "Relationship" and "Deal".

9.9 Maximum concern for "Relationship" and "Deal". This is achieved by preparation, searching for mutual benefit positions, commitment to achieving the best possible solution for both parties.

CHAPTER 23

Conclusion

I STARTED THIS BOOK with the paradox of Christian organisations—that is that we should be very good at relationships and be highly united but in fact this is often not the case. Having said this, I think it is true that because of our common faith and belief, we are united as families. In view of this, Christian bodies have the potential to be outstanding in terms of the people side of things. We can be strong in relationships, act in unity and have a strong resolve to carry out kingdom building work together.

In order to achieve this, we have to only tackle a few things that are fairly self-evident. Amongst these are having real relationships, accepting accountability, being united and aligned in our purpose, being humble and not expecting our agenda to dominate. We also need to use the right talents in the right areas and demonstrate a high degree of resolve in serving our faith.

If these things are fairly evident, what else is it that holds us back from building the very best and most admired organisations on the planet? Well, one thought I would like to leave you with is that whilst it is fairly easy to identify what we should do, it is much harder to do it. Resolving the people issues means that we, both leaders and led, have to change. We have to be willing to operate as our 'better selves' at all times and not fall into doing the things we all do, like wanting our own way, wanting to dominate, wanting to have lots of recognition and wanting our needs to be met before those of our wider Christian family.

To operate as our better selves we do need to set the right example, inspire or support a healthy vision for the organisation, search for new and better ways of doing things, foster collaboration and celebrate the contribution of others. It is also better to give than to receive so let's genuinely see how we can encourage, love and support our brothers and sisters in Christ in a joyous and genuine way.

It may sound pretty tough, and exhausting, to try and be our better selves all the time—it's probably going to take a lot of prayer and a culture that values this kind of positive behaviour and is not receptive to negativity, gossip and verbal slight. It also means we have to try out positive techniques, be willing to give new relationships a chance and, even more crucially, be willing to start some old relationships afresh. We have to leave some of the baggage we have about people at the door and try and make sure we find out who they really are and not who we think they are.

I have a really good friend who has many strong points, he's very bright, interesting and most of all courageous and cool headed when facing really tough challenges and unusual pressures. However, he does one thing that is not so great and, having talked it through, he decided to address this. The one thing is that he decides very quickly who are the good and bad guys in his world, and he then almost never changes his mind. As in the old Westerns, people are allocated white or black hats and this happens pretty quickly. Once he's allocated the hat, it is almost impossible to get him to change his view. The good guys stay the good guys, pretty much no matter what they do, and the bad guys can never change their status. In fact he continually looks for material, in the form of behaviour, to reinforce his view. His view then of course becomes a self-fulfilling prophecy. We need to be careful we don't adopt this approach with those around us and those we serve alongside in our organisations.

I have sought to provide some models and case studies in this book so you can better examine your own situations, see what's relevant and apply some solutions to the challenges you face. However, the really hard part of this is having the will to try out these techniques and put them into practice, followed by the consistency needed to ensure that you give these changes a chance to work. Hopefully a lot of this will be fun, but a lot of it will also need commitment and hard work. A good way of tackling this will be to encourage one another as you seek to address any issues which you feel your organisation might have—'Therefore encourage one another and build each other up, just as in fact you are doing' (1 Thess 5:11).

Bibliography

Warren, R.—The Purpose Driven Church (Zondervan, 1995)

Hybels, B.—Axiom (Zondervan, 2008)

Adams, D.—Hitchhiker's Guide to the Galaxy (Harmony, 1994)

Collins, J.—Good to Great (Random House, 2001)

Buckingham, M. & Coffman, K.—First Break All the Rules (Simon & Schuster, 1999)

Showkeir, J. & M.—Authentic Conversations (Berrett-Koehler Publishers, 2008)

Gladwell, M.—Tipping Point (Abacus, 2001)

Lencioni, P.—The Five Dysfunctions of a Team (Jossey-Bass, 2002)

Scott, S.—Fierce Conversations (Berkley Trade, 2004)

Handy, C.—Understanding Voluntary Organisations (Penguin UK, 1999)

Ury, W.—Getting Past No (Random House, 1991)

Buffett, M. & Clark, D.—Warren Buffet's Management Secrets (Simon & Schuster, 2010)

Printed in Great Britain
by Amazon.co.uk, Ltd.,
Marston Gate.